S0-BYQ-127

Corner House Publishers

SOCIAL SCIENCE REPRINTS

General Editor MAURICE FILLER

DANIEL BOONE.

From the portrait by Chester Harding made in 1819, when Boone was eighty-five years old. (See pp. 237–239.)

Daniel Boone

BY

REUBEN GOLD THWAITES

Author of "Father Marquette," "The Colonies, 1492-1750," "Down Historic Waterways," "Afloat on the Ohio," etc.; Editor of "The Jesuit Relations and Allied Documents," "Chronicles of Border Warfare," "Wisconsin Historical Collections," etc.

Illustrated

CORNER HOUSE PUBLISHERS

WILLIAMSTOWN, MASSACHUSETTS 01267

1977

REPRINTED 1977

BY

CORNER HOUSE PUBLISHERS

ISBN 0–87928–084–0

Printed in the United States of America

TO THE MEMORY OF THE LATE

LYMAN COPELAND DRAPER, LL.D.

WHOSE UNPARALLELED COLLECTION OF MANUSCRIPT MATERIALS FOR WESTERN HISTORY IN THE LIBRARY OF THE WISCONSIN STATE HISTORICAL SOCIETY HAS MADE PRACTICABLE THE PREPARATION OF THIS LITTLE BOOK

PREFACE

Poets, historians, and orators have for a hundred years sung the praises of Daniel Boone as the typical backwoodsman of the trans-Alleghany region. Despite popular belief, he was not really the founder of Kentucky. Other explorers and hunters had been there long before him; he himself was piloted through Cumberland Gap by John Finley; and his was not even the first permanent settlement in Kentucky, for Harrodsburg preceded it by nearly a year; his services in defense of the West, during nearly a half century of border warfare, were not comparable to those of George Rogers Clark or Benjamin Logan; as a commonwealth builder he was surpassed by several. Nevertheless, Boone's picturesque career possesses a romantic and even pathetic interest that can never fail to charm the student of history. He was great as a hunter, explorer, surveyor, and land-pilot—probably he found few equals as a rifleman; no man on the border knew Indians more thoroughly or fought them more skilfully than he; his life was filled to the brim with perilous adventures. He was not a man of affairs, he did not understand the art of money-getting, and he lost his lands because, although a surveyor, he was careless of legal forms of entry. He fled before the advance of the civilization which he had ushered in: from Pennsylvania, wandering with his parents to North Carolina in search of broader lands; thence into Kentucky because the Carolina borders were crowded; then to the Kanawha Valley, for the reason that Kentucky was being settled too fast to suit his fancy; lastly to far-off Missouri, in order, as he said, to get "elbow room." Experiences similar to his have made misanthropes of many another man—like Clark, for instance; but the temperament of this honest, silent, nature-loving man only mellowed with age; his closing years were radiant with the sunshine of serene content and the dimly appreciated consciousness of world-wide fame; and he died full of years, in heart a simple hunter to the last—although he had also served with credit as magistrate, soldier, and legislator. At his death the Constitutional Convention of Missouri went into mourning for twenty days, and the State of Kentucky claimed his bones, and has erected over them a suitable monument.

There have been published many lives of Boone, but none of them in recent years. Had the late Dr. Lyman Copeland Draper, of Wisconsin, ever written the huge biography for which he gathered materials throughout a lifetime of laborious collection, those volumes—there were to be several—would doubtless have uttered the last possible word concerning the famous Kentucky pioneer. Draper's manuscript, however, never advanced beyond a few chapters; but the raw materials which he gathered for this work, and for many others of like character, are now in the library of the Wisconsin State Historical Society, available to all scholars. From this almost inexhaustible treasure-house the present writer has obtained the bulk of his information, and has had the advantage of being able to consult numerous critical notes made by his dear and learned friend. A book so small as this, concerning a character every phase of whose career was replete with thrilling incident, would doubtless not have won the approbation of Dr. Draper, whose unaccomplished biographical plans were all drawn upon a large scale; but we are living in a busy age, and life is brief—condensation is the necessary order of the day. It will always be a source of regret that Draper's projected literary monument to Boone was not completed for the press, although its bulk would have been forbidding to any but specialists, who would have sought its pages as a cyclopedia of Western border history.

Through the courtesy both of Colonel Reuben T. Durrett, of Louisville, President of the Filson Club, and of Mrs. Ranck, we are permitted to include among our illustrations reproductions of some of the plates in the late George W. Ranck's stately monograph upon Boonesborough. Aid in tracing original portraits of Boone has been received from Mrs. Jennie C. Morton and General

Fayette Hewitt, of Frankfort; Miss Marjory Dawson and Mr. W. G. Lackey, of St. Louis; Mr. William H. King, of Winnetka, Ill.; and Mr. J. Marx Etting, of Philadelphia.

R. G. T.

MADISON, WIS., *1902*.

CONTENTS

LIST OF ILLUSTRATIONS

DANIEL BOONE

CHAPTER I

ANCESTRY AND TRAINING

THE grandfather of Daniel Boone—George by name—was born in 1666 at the peaceful little hamlet of Stoak, near the city of Exeter, in Devonshire, England. His father had been a blacksmith; but he himself acquired the weaver's art. In due time George married Mary Maugridge, a young woman three years his junior, and native of the neighboring village of Bradninch, whither he had gone to follow his trade. This worthy couple, professed Quakers, became the parents of nine children, all born in Bradninch—George, Sarah, Squire,* Mary, John, Joseph, Benjamin, James, and Samuel. All of

* Not an abbreviation of "esquire," as has been supposed, but given because of some old family connection. This name was transmitted through several generations of Boones.

these, except John, married, and left numerous descendants in America.

The elder Boones were ambitious for the welfare of their large family. They were also fretful under the bitter intolerance encountered by Quakers in those unrestful times. As the children grew to maturity, the enterprising weaver sought information regarding the colony which his coreligionist William Penn had, some thirty years previous, established in America, where were promised cheap lands, religious freedom, political equality, and exact justice to all men. There were then no immigration bureaus to encourage and instruct those who proposed settling in America; no news-letters from traveling correspondents, to tell the people at home about the Western world; or books or pamphlets illustrating the country. The only method which occurred to George Boone, of Bradninch, by which he could satisfy himself regarding the possibilities of Pennsylvania as a future home for his household, was to send out some of his older children as prospectors.

Accordingly—somewhere about 1712–14,

family tradition says—young George (aged from twenty-two to twenty-four years), Sarah (a year and a half younger), and Squire (born November 25, 1696) were despatched to the promised land, and spent several months in its inspection. Leaving Sarah and Squire in Pennsylvania, George returned to his parents with a favorable report.

On the seventeenth of August, 1717, the Boones, parents and children, bade a sorrowful but brave farewell to their relatives and friends in old Bradninch, whom they were never again to see. After journeying some eighty miles over rugged country to the port of Bristol, they there entered a sailing vessel bound for Philadelphia, where they safely arrived upon the tenth of October.

Philadelphia was then but a village. Laid out like a checker-board, with architecture of severe simplicity, its best residences were surrounded by gardens and orchards. The town was substantial, neat, and had the appearance of prosperity; but the frontier was not far away—beyond outlying fields the untamed forest closed in upon the little capital.

The fur trade flourished but two or three days' journey into the forest, and Indians were frequently seen upon the streets. When, therefore, the Boones decided to settle in what is now Abingdon, twelve or fourteen miles north of the town, in a sparse neighborhood of Quaker farmers, they at once became backwoodsmen, such as they remained for the rest of their lives.

They were, however, not long in Abingdon. Soon after, we find them domiciled a few miles to the northwest in the little frontier hamlet of North Wales, in Gwynedd township; this was a Welsh community whose members had, a few years before, turned Quakers.

Sarah Boone appears, about this time, to have married one Jacob Stover, a German who settled in Oley township, now in Berks County. The elder George Boone, now that he had become accustomed to moving, after his long, quiet years as a Devonshire weaver, appears to have made small ado over folding his family tent and seeking other pastures. In 1718 he took out a warrant for four hundred acres of land in Oley, and near the close of the following year removed to his daughter's neighborhood. This time he settled in earnest, for here in Oley—or rather the later subdivision thereof called Exeter—he spent the remainder of his days, dying in his original log cabin there, in 1744, at the age of seventy-eight. He left eight children, fifty-two grandchildren, and ten great-grandchildren—in all, seventy descendants: Devonshire men, Germans, Welsh, and Scotch-Irish amalgamated into a sturdy race of American pioneers.

Among the early Welsh Quakers in the rustic neighborhood of North Wales were the Morgans. On the twenty-third of July, 1720, at the Gwynedd meeting-house, in accordance with the Quaker ceremony, Squire Boone married Sarah Morgan, daughter of John. A descendant tells us that at this time "Squire Boone was a man of rather small stature, fair complexion, red hair, and gray eyes; while his wife was a woman something over the common size, strong and active, with black hair and eyes, and raised in the Quaker order."

For ten or eleven years Squire and Sarah

Boone lived in Gwynedd township, probably on rented land, the former adding to their small income by occasional jobs of weaving, for he had learned his father's trade. They were thrifty folk, but it took ten years under these primitive conditions to accumulate even the small sum sufficient to acquire a farm of their own. Toward the close of the year 1730, Squire obtained for a modest price a grant of 250 acres of land situated in his father's township, Oley—a level tract adapted to grazing purposes, on Owatin Creek, some eight miles southeast of the present city of Reading, and a mile and a half from Exeter meeting-house. Here, probably early in 1731, the Boones removed with their four children. Relatives and Quaker neighbors assisted, after the manner of the frontier, in erecting a log cabin for the new-comers and in clearing and fencing for them a small patch of ground.

In this rude backwoods home, in the valley of the Schuylkill, was born, upon the second of November (new style), 1734, Daniel Boone, fourth son and sixth child of Squire and Sarah. It is thought that the name

Daniel was suggested by that of Daniel Boone, a well-known Dutch painter who had died in London in 1698, "and who may have been known, or distantly related, to the family." The other children were: Sarah (born in 1724), Israel (1726), Samuel (1728), Jonathan (1730), Elizabeth (1732), Mary (1736), George (1739), Edward (1744), Squire, and Hannah, all of them natives of Oley.*

Born into a frontier community, Daniel Boone's entire life was spent amid similar surroundings, varying only in degree. With the sight of Indians he was from the first familiar. They frequently visited Oley and Exeter, and were cordially received by the Quakers. George Boone's house was the scene of many a friendly gathering of the tribesmen. When Daniel was eight years of age, the celebrated Moravian missionary, Count Zinzendorf, held a synod in a barn at Oley, a party of converted Delaware Indians, who preached in favor of Christianity, being

* Edward was killed by Indians when thirty-six years old, and Squire died at the age of seventy-six. Their brothers and sisters lived to ages varying from eighty-three to ninety-one.

the principal attractions at this meeting. Thus young Boone started in life with an accurate knowledge of the American savage, which served him well during his later years of adventurous exploration and settlement-building.

Squire Boone appears soon to have become a leader in his community. His farm, to whose acres he from time to time added, was attended to as closely as was usual among the frontiersmen of his day; and at home the business of weaving was not neglected, for he kept in frequent employment five or six looms, making "homespun" cloths for his neighbors and the market. He had an excellent grazing range some five or six miles north of the homestead, and each season sent his stock thither, as was the custom at that time. Mrs. Boone and Daniel accompanied the cows, and from early spring until late in autumn lived in a rustic cabin, far from any other human beings. Hard by, over a cool spring, was a dairy-house, in which the stout-armed mother made and kept her butter and cheese; while her favorite boy watched the herd as, led by their bell-carriers, they roamed at will through the woods, his duty at sunset being to drive them to the cabin for milking, and later to lock them for the night within the cow-pens, secure from wild animals or prowling cattle-thieves.

While tending his cattle, a work involving abundant leisure, the young herdsman was also occupied in acquiring the arts of the forest. For the first two or three years—his pastoral life having commenced at the tender age of ten—his only weapon was a slender, smoothly shaved sapling, with a small bunch of gnarled roots at the end, in throwing which he grew so expert as easily to kill birds and other small game. When reaching the dignity of a dozen years, his father bought him a rifle, with which he soon became an unerring marksman. But, although he henceforth provided wild meat enough for the family, his passion for hunting sometimes led him to neglect the cattle, which were allowed to stray far from home and pass the night in the deep forest.

Soon each summer of herding came to be succeeded by a winter's hunt. In this occupation the boy roved far and wide over the

Neversink mountain-range to the north and west of Monocacy Valley, killing and curing game for the family, and taking the skins to Philadelphia, where he exchanged them for articles needed in the chase—long hunting-knives, and flints, lead, and powder for his gun.

In those days the children of the frontier grew up with but slight store of such education as is obtainable from books. The open volume of nature, however, they carefully conned. The ways of the wilderness they knew full well—concerning the storms and floods, the trees and hills, the wild animals and the Indians, they were deeply learned; well they knew how to live alone in the forest, and to thrive happily although surrounded by a thousand lurking dangers. This quiet, mild-mannered, serious-faced Quaker youth, Daniel Boone, was an ardent lover of the wild woods and their inhabitants, which he knew as did Audubon and Thoreau; but of regular schooling he had none. When he was about fourteen years of age, his brother Samuel, nearly seven years his senior, married Sarah Day, an intelligent young Quakeress who had more education than was customary in this neighborhood. Sarah taught Daniel the elements of "the three R's." To this knowledge he added somewhat by later self-teaching, so that as a man he could read understandingly, do rough surveying, keep notes of his work, and write a sensible although badly spelled letter—for our backwoods hero was, in truth, no scholar, although as well equipped in this direction as were most of his fellows.

In time Squire Boone, a man of enterprise and vigor, added blacksmithing to his list of occupations, and employed his young sons in this lusty work. Thus Daniel served, for a time, as a worker in iron as well as a hunter and herdsman; although it was noticed that his art was chiefly developed in the line of making and mending whatever pertained to traps and guns. He was a fearless rider of his father's horses; quick, though bred a Quaker, to resent what he considered wrong treatment;* true to his

* Indeed, it is a matter of record that other members also of this stout-hearted Devonshire family were "sometimes rather too belligerent and self-willed," and had "occasion-

young friends; fond of long, solitary tramps through the dark forest, or of climbing hill-tops for bird's-eye views of the far-stretching wilderness. Effective training this, for the typical pioneer of North America.

---

ally to be dealt with by the meeting." Daniel's oldest sister, Sarah, married a man who was not a Quaker, and consequently she was "disowned" by the society. His oldest brother, Israel, also married a worldling and was similarly treated; and their father, who countenanced Israel's disloyal act and would not retract his error, was in 1748 likewise expelled.

CHAPTER II

THE NIMROD OF THE YADKIN

THE lofty barrier of the Alleghany Mountains was of itself sufficient to prevent the pioneers of Pennsylvania from wandering far westward. Moreover, the Indians beyond these hills were fiercer than those with whom the Quakers were familiar; their occasional raids to the eastward, through the mountain passes, won for them a reputation which did not incline the border farmers to cultivate their further acquaintance. To the southwest, however, there were few obstacles to the spread of settlement. For several hundred miles the Appalachians run in parallel ranges from northeast to southwest—from Pennsylvania, through Virginia, West Virginia, the Carolinas, and east Tennessee, until at last they degenerate into scattered foot-hills upon the Georgia plain. Through the long, deep troughs between these ranges—notably in the famous Valley of Virginia between the Blue Ridge and the Alleghanies —Pennsylvanians freely wandered into the south and southwest, whenever possessed by thirst for new and broader lands. Hostile Indians sometimes penetrated these great valleys and brought misery in their train; but the work of pioneering along this path was less arduous than had the western mountains been scaled at a time when the colonists were still few and weak.

Between the years 1732 and 1750, numerous groups of Pennsylvanians—Germans and Irish largely, with many Quakers among them—had been wending their way through the mountain troughs, and gradually pushing forward the line of settlement, until now it had reached the upper waters of the Yadkin River, in the northwest corner of North Carolina. Trials abundant fell to their lot; but the soil of the valleys was unusually fertile, game was abundant, the climate mild, the country beautiful, and life in general upon the new frontier, although rough, such as to appeal to the borderers as a thing desirable. The glowing reports of each new group attracted others. Thus was the wilderness tamed by a steady stream of immigration from the older lands of the northern colonies, while not a few penetrated to this Arcadia through the passes of the Blue Ridge, from eastern Virginia and the Carolinas.

Squire and Sarah Boone, of Oley, now possessed eleven children, some of whom were married and settled within this neighborhood which consisted so largely of the Boones and their relatives. The choicest lands of eastern Pennsylvania had at last been located. The outlook for the younger Boones, who soon would need new homesteads, did not appear encouraging. The fame of the Yadkin Valley, five hundred miles southwestward, had reached Oley, and thither, in the spring of 1750, the majority of the Boones, after selling their lands and surplus stock, bravely took up the line of march.*

With the women and children stowed in canvas-covered wagons, the men and boys riding their horses at front and rear, and driving the lagging cattle, the picturesque little caravan slowly found its way to the

* John and James remained, and lived and died in Oley.

ford at Harper's Ferry, thence up the beautiful valley of the Shenandoah. By night they pitched their camps beside some gurgling spring, gathered the animals within the circle of the wagons, and, with sentinel posted against possible surprises by Indians, sat around the blazing fire to discuss the experiences of the day—Daniel, as the hunter for the party, doubtless having the most interesting adventures of them all.

Tradition has it that the Boones tarried by the way, for a year or more, on Linnville Creek, six miles north of Harrisonburg, in Rockingham County, Va. In any event, they appear to have resumed their journey by the autumn of 1751. Pushing on through the Valley of Virginia—an undulating, heavily forested table-land from three to ten miles in width—they forded the upper waters of numerous rivers, some of which, according to the tilt of the land, flow eastward and southeastward toward the Atlantic, and others westward and southwestward toward the Ohio. This is one of the fairest and most salubrious regions in America; but they did not again stop until the promised land of the Yadkin was reached.

The country was before them, to choose from it practically what they would. Between the Yadkin and the Catawba there was a broad expanse of elevated prairie, yielding a luxuriant growth of grass, while the bottoms skirting the numerous streams were thick-grown to canebrake. Here were abundant meadows for the cattle, fish and game and wild fruits in quantity quite exceeding young Daniel's previous experience, a well-tempered climate, and to the westward a mountain-range which cast long afternoon shadows over the plain and spoke eloquently of untamed dominions beyond. Out of this land of plenty Squire Boone chose a claim at Buffalo Lick, where Dutchman's Creek joins with the North Fork of Yadkin.

Daniel was now a lad of eighteen. Nominally, he helped in the working of his father's farm and in the family smithy; actually, he was more often in the woods with his long rifle. At first, buffaloes were so plenty that a party of three or four men, with dogs, could kill from ten to twenty in a day; but soon the sluggish animals receded before the advance of white men, hiding themselves behind the mountain wall. An ordinary hunter could slaughter four or five deer in a day; in the autumn, he might from sunrise to sunset shoot enough bears to provide over a ton of bear-bacon for winter use; wild turkeys were easy prey; beavers, otters, and muskrats abounded; while wolves, panthers, and wildcats overran the country. Overcome by his passion for the chase, our young Nimrod soon began to spend months at a time in the woods, especially in autumn and winter. He found also more profit in this occupation than at either the forge or the plow; for at their nearest market town, Salisbury, twenty miles away, good prices were paid for skins, which were regularly shipped thence to the towns upon the Atlantic coast.

The Catawba Indians lived about sixty miles distant, and the Cherokees still farther. These tribesmen not infrequently visited the thinly scattered settlement on the Yadkin, seeking trade with the whites, with whom they were as yet on good terms. They were, however, now and then raided by Northern Indians, particularly the Shawnese, who, collecting in the Valley of Virginia, swept down upon them with fury; sometimes also committing depredations upon the whites who had befriended their tribal enemies, and who unfortunately had staked their farms in the old-time war-path of the marauders.

In the year 1754, the entire American border, from the Yadkin to the St. Lawrence, became deeply concerned in the Indian question. France and England had long been rivals for the mastery of the North American continent lying west of the Alleghanies. France had established a weak chain of posts upon the upper Great Lakes, and down the Mississippi River to New Orleans, thus connecting Canada with Louisiana. In the Valley of the Ohio, however, without which the French could not long hold the Western country, there was a protracted rivalry between French and English fur-traders, each seeking to supplant the intruding foreigner. This led to the outbreak of the French and Indian War, which was waged vigorously for five years, until New France fell, and the

English obtained control of all Canada and that portion of the continent lying between the Atlantic Ocean and the Mississippi.

As early as 1748, backwoodsmen from Pennsylvania had made a small settlement on New River, just west of the Alleghanies—a settlement which the Boones must have visited, as it lay upon the road to the Yadkin; and in the same season several adventurous Virginians hunted and made land-claims in Kentucky and Tennessee. In the following year there was formed for Western fur trading and colonizing purposes, the Ohio Company, composed of wealthy Virginians, among them two brothers of George Washington. In 1753 French soldiers built a little log fort on French Creek, a tributary of the Alleghany; and, despite Virginia's protest, delivered by young Major Washington, were planning to erect another at the forks of the Ohio, where Pittsburg now is. Thither Washington went, in the succeeding year, with a body of Virginia militiamen, to construct an English stockade at the forks; but the French defeated him in the Great Meadows hard by and themselves erected the fort.

The Nimrod of the Yadkin

It is thought by some writers that young Boone, then twenty years of age, served in the Pennsylvania militia which protected the frontier from the Indian forays which succeeded this episode. A year later (1755) the inexperienced General Braddock, fresh from England, set out, with Washington upon his staff, to teach a lesson to these Frenchmen who had intruded upon land claimed by the colony of Virginia.

In Braddock's little army were a hundred North Carolina frontiersmen, under Captain Hugh Waddell; their wagoner and blacksmith was Daniel Boone. His was one of those heavily laden baggage-wagons which, history tells us, greatly impeded the progress of the English, and contributed not a little to the terrible disaster which overtook the column in the ravine of Turtle Creek, only a few miles from Pittsburg. The baggage-train was the center of a fierce attack from Indians, led by French officers, and many drivers were killed. Young Boone, however, cut the traces of his team, and mounting a horse, fortunately escaped by flight. Behind him the Indian allies of the French, now unchecked, laid waste the panic-stricken frontiers of Pennsylvania and Virginia. But the Yadkin, which Boone soon reached, was as yet unscarred; the Northern tribes were busied in the tide of intercolonial warfare, and the Catawbas and Cherokees thus far remained steadfast to their old-time promises of peace.

Daniel was now a man, full-grown. He had brought home with him not only some knowledge of what war meant, but his imagination had become heated by a new passion —the desire to explore as well as to hunt. While upon the campaign he had fallen in with another adventurous soul, John Finley by name, who fired his heart with strange tales of lands and game to the west of the mountains. Finley was a Scotch-Irishman of roving tendencies, who had emigrated to Pennsylvania and joined a colony of his compatriots. As early as 1752 he had become a fur-trader. In the course of his rambles many perilous adventures befell him in the Kentucky wilds, into which he had penetrated as far as the Falls of the Ohio, where Louisville is now built. Hurrying, with other woodsmen, to Braddock's support, he enrolled himself under George Croghan, a famous trader to the Indians. But the expert services of Croghan and his men, who, well understanding the methods of savages upon the war-path, offered to serve as scouts, were coldly rejected by Braddock, who soon had occasion to regret that he had not taken their advice.

Finley found in the Yadkin wagoner a kindred spirit, and suggested to him with eagerness a method of reaching Kentucky by following the trail of the buffaloes and the Shawnese, northwestward through Cumberland Gap. To reach this hunter's paradise, to which Finley had pointed the way, was now Boone's daily dream.

CHAPTER III

LIFE ON THE BORDER

It was many years before Daniel Boone realized his dream of reaching Kentucky. Such an expedition into the far-off wilderness could not be lightly undertaken; its hardships and dangers were innumerable; and the way thither from the forks of the Yadkin was not as easily found, through this perplexing tangle of valleys and mountains, as Finley had supposed. His own route had doubtless been over the Ohio Company's pass from the upper waters of the Potomac to a tributary of the Monongahela.

Another reason caused Daniel long to linger near his home. A half-dozen years before the Boones reached the Yadkin country there had located here a group of several related families, the Bryans, originally from Ireland. Pennsylvanians at first, they had, as neighbors crowded them, drifted southwestward into the Valley of Virginia;

and finally, keeping well ahead of other settlers, established themselves at the forks of the Yadkin. They took kindly to the Boones, the two groups intermarried, and both were in due course pioneers of Kentucky. Rebecca, the daughter of Joseph Bryan, was fifteen years of age when Daniel first read his fate in her shining black eyes. In the spring following his return from Braddock's slaughter-pen he led her to the altar, the ceremony being performed by old Squire Boone—farmer, weaver, blacksmith, and now justice of the peace for Rowan County.

An historian of the border, who had studied well the family traditions, thus describes Daniel and Rebecca at the time when they set forth together upon the journey of life: "Behold that young man, exhibiting such unusual firmness and energy of character, five feet eight inches in height, with broad chest and shoulders, his form gradually tapering downward to his extremities; his hair moderately black; blue eyes arched with yellowish eyebrows; his lips thin, with a mouth peculiarly wide; a countenance fair and ruddy, with a nose a little bordering on the

Roman order. Such was Daniel Boone, now past twenty-one, presenting altogether a noble, manly, prepossessing appearance. . . . Rebecca Bryan, whose brow had now been fanned by the breezes of seventeen summers, was, like Rebecca of old, 'very fair to look upon,' with jet-black hair and eyes, complexion rather dark, and something over the common size of her sex; her whole demeanor expressive of her childlike artlessness, pleasing in her address, and unaffectedly kind in all her deportment. Never was there a more gentle, affectionate, forbearing creature than this same fair youthful bride of the Yadkin." In the annals of the frontier, as elsewhere, all brides are fair and grooms are manly; but, allowing for the natural enthusiasm of hero-worshipers, we may, from the abundance of testimony to that effect, at least conclude that Daniel and Rebecca Boone were a well-favored couple, fit to rear a family of sturdy borderers.

It was neither the day nor the place for expensive trousseaus and wedding journeys. After a hilarious wedding-feast, Boone and his wife, with scanty equipment, immediately commenced their hard task of winning a livelihood from the soil and the forest. At first occupying a rude log cabin in his father's yard, they soon afterward acquired some level land of their own, lying upon Sugar Tree, a tributary of Dutchman's Creek, in the Bryan settlement, a few miles north of Squire Boone's. All of this neighborhood lies within what is now Davie County, still one of the richest farming districts in North Carolina. Save when driven out by Indian alarms and forays, they here lived quietly for many years.

The pioneers in the then back country, along the eastern foot-hills of the Alleghanies, led a rough, primitive life, such as is hardly possible to-day, when there is no longer any frontier within the United States, and but few districts are so isolated as to be more than two or three days' journey from a railway. Most of them, however, had been bred, as were the Boones and the Bryans, to the rude experiences of the border. With slight knowledge of books, they were accustomed to living in the simplest manner, and from childhood were inured to the hardships and privations incident to great distance from the centers of settlement; they possessed the virtues of hospitality and neighborliness, and were hardy, rugged, honest-hearted folk, admirably suited to their self-appointed task of forcing back the walls of savagery, in order that civilization might cover the land. We may well honor them for the great service that they rendered to mankind.

The dress of a backwoodsman like Daniel Boone was a combination of Indian and civilized attire. A long hunting-shirt, of coarse cloth or of dressed deerskins, sometimes with an ornamental collar, was his principal garment; drawers and leggings of like material were worn; the feet were encased in moccasins of deerskin—soft and pliant, but cold in winter, even when stuffed with deer's hair or dry leaves, and so spongy as to be no protection against wet feet, which made every hunter an early victim to rheumatism. Hanging from the belt, which girt the hunting-shirt, were the powder-horn, bullet-pouch, scalping-knife, and tomahawk; while the breast of the shirt served as a generous pocket for food when the hunter or warrior was upon the trail. For head-covering, the favorite was a soft cap of coonskin, with the bushy tail dangling behind; but Boone himself despised this gear, and always wore a hat. The women wore huge sunbonnets and loose gowns of home-made cloth; they generally went barefoot in summer, but wore moccasins in winter.

Daniel Boone's cabin was a simple box of logs, reared in "cob-house" style, the chinks stuffed with moss and clay, with a door and perhaps but a single window. Probably there was but one room below, with a low attic under the rafters, reached by a ladder. A great outside chimney, built either of rough stones or of small logs, coated on the inside with clay mortar and carefully chinked with the same, was built against one end of this rude house. In the fireplace, large enough for logs five or six feet in length, there was a crane from which was hung the iron pot in which the young wife cooked simple meals of corn-mush, pumpkins, squashes, beans, potatoes, and pork, or wild meat of many kinds, fresh and dried; in a bake-kettle, laid upon the live coals, she made the bread and corn pone, or fried her steaks, which added variety to the fare.

Dishes and other utensils were few—some pewter plates, forks, and spoons; wooden bowls and trenchers, with gourds and hard-shelled squashes for drinking-mugs. For knife, Boone doubtless used his belt-weapon, and scorned the crock plates, now slowly creeping into the valley, as calculated to dull its edge. Over the fireplace deer's horns served as rests for his gun. Into the log wall were driven great wooden pegs, hanging from which flitches of dried and smoked bacon, venison, and bear's-meat mingled freely with the family's scanty wardrobe.

With her cooking and rude mending, her moccasin-making, her distaff and loom for making cloths, her occasional plying of the hoe in the small vegetable patch, and her ever-present care of the children and dairy, Rebecca Boone was abundantly occupied.

In these early years of married life Daniel proved a good husbandman, planting and garnering his crops with regularity, and pasturing a few scrawny cattle and swine upon the wild lands adjoining his farm. Doubt-

BOONE'S POWDER-HORN AND BAKE-KETTLE.

In possession of Wisconsin State Historical Society. The horn once belonged to Daniel's brother Israel, and bears the initials "I B".

less at times he did smithy-work for the neighbors and took a hand at the loom, as had his father and grandfather before him. Sometimes he was engaged with his wagon in the caravans which each autumn found their way from the Yadkin and the other mountain valleys down to the Atlantic cities, carrying furs to market; it was as yet too early in the history of the back country for the cattle-raisers to send their animals to the coast. In the Valley of Virginia, hemmed in upon the east by the Blue Ridge, packhorses were alone used in this traffic, for the mountain paths were rough and narrow; but wagons could be utilized in the more southern districts. The caravans brought back to the pioneers salt, iron, cloths, and a few other manufactured goods. This annual expedition over, Boone was free to go upon long hunts in the forest, where he cured great stores of meat for his family and prepared the furs for market.

The backwoodsmen of the Yadkin had few machines to assist them in their labor, and these were of the simplest sort. Practically, every settler was his own mechanic—

although some men became, in certain lines, more expert than their neighbors, and to them fell such work for the entire settlement. Grinding corn into meal, or cracking it into hominy, were, as usual with primitive peoples, tasks involving the most machinery. Rude mortars and pestles, some of the latter ingeniously worked by means of springy "sweeps," were commonly seen; a device something like a nutmeg-grater was often used when the corn was soft; two circular millstones, worked by hand, were effective, and there were some operated by water-power.

Medicine was at a crude stage, many of the so-called cures being as old as Egypt, while others were borrowed from the Indians. The borderers firmly believed in the existence of witches; bad dreams, eclipses of the sun, the howling of dogs, and the croaking of ravens, were sure to bring disasters in their train.

Their sports laid stress on physical accomplishments — great strength, dexterity with the rifle, hunting, imitating the calls of wild birds and beasts, throwing the tomahawk, running, jumping, wrestling, dancing, and horse-racing; they were also fond, as they gathered around one another's great fireplaces in the long winter evenings, of story-telling and dramatic recitation. Some of the wealthier members of this primitive society owned negro slaves, to whom, sometimes, they were cruel, freely using the whip upon both women and men. Indeed, in their own frequent quarrels fierce brutality was sometimes used, adversaries in a fist-fight being occasionally maimed or otherwise disfigured for life.

There was, for a long time, "neither law nor gospel" upon this far-away frontier. Justices of the peace had small authority. Preachers were at first unknown. Many of the borderers were Presbyterians, and others Quakers; but under such social conditions these were little else than names. Nevertheless, there was a sound public sentiment among these rude, isolated people, who were a law unto themselves. They respected and honored candor, honesty, hospitality, regular habits, and good behavior generally; and very severe were the punishments with which they visited offenders. If a man acted as a coward in time of war, shirked his full measure of duty to the public, failed to care for his family, was careless about his debts, stole from his neighbors, was needlessly profane, or failed to treat women respectfully, he was either shunned by his fellows or forced to leave the settlement.

Amid such surroundings and of such stuff was Daniel Boone in the days when he was living uneventfully in the valley of the Yadkin as farmer, blacksmith, wagoner, and hunter, before the Indian wars and his explorations west of the long-shadowed mountain-range made of him a popular hero.

CHAPTER IV

RED MAN AGAINST WHITE MAN

THE borderers in the Valley of Virginia and on the western highlands of the Carolinas were largely engaged in raising horses, cattle, sheep, and hogs, which grazed at will upon the broad slopes of the eastern foothills of the Alleghanies, most of them being in as wild a state as the great roving herds now to be seen upon the semi-arid plains of the far West. Indeed, there are some strong points of resemblance between the life of the frontier herdsman of the middle of the eighteenth century and that of the "cow" ranchers of our own day, although the most primitive conditions now existing would have seemed princely to Daniel Boone. The annual round-up, the branding of young stock, the sometimes deadly disputes between herdsmen, and the autumnal drive to market, are features in common.

With the settlement of the valleys and the

steady increase in the herds, it was necessary each season to find new pastures. Thus the herdsmen pushed farther and farther into the wilderness to the south and west, and actually crossed the mountains at many points. Even before the arrival of the Boones, the Bryans had frequently, toward the end of summer, as the lower pastures thinned, driven their stock to a distance of sixty and seventy miles to green valleys lying between the western buttresses of the mountain wall.

This gradual pressure upon the hunting-grounds of the Cherokees and the Catawbas was not unnoticed by the tribesmen. There had long been heard deep mutterings, especially by the former, who were well-disposed toward the ever-meddling French; but until the year of Daniel Boone's wedding the southern frontiers had not known an Indian uprising.

The year previous (1755) the Cherokees had given reluctant permission to the whites to build two posts in their country for the protection of the frontiers against the French, who, with their Indian allies, were continually active against the New York, Pennsylvania, and Virginia frontiers, and were known to be attempting the corruption of the Southern Indians. Fort Prince George was accordingly erected upon the Savannah River, and Fort Loudon upon the Tennessee. In 1756 Fort Dobbs was constructed a short distance south of the South Fork of the Yadkin. These three centers of refuge were upon the extreme southwestern borders of the English colonies.

These "forts" of the American border would have proved slight defenses in the presence of an enemy armed with even the lightest artillery, but were generally sufficient to withstand a foe possessing only muskets and rifles. Fort Dobbs was an oblong space forty-three by fifty-three feet, girt by walls about twelve feet high, consisting of double rows of logs standing on end; earth dug from the ditch which surrounded the fort was piled against the feet of these palisades, inside and out, to steady them; they were fastened to one another by wooden pins, and their tops were sharpened so as to impede those who might seek to climb over. At the angles of the stockade were blockhouses three stories high, each story projecting about eighteen inches beyond the one beneath; there were openings in the floors of the two upper stories to enable the defenders to fire down upon an enemy which sought to enter below. Along the inside of one, or perhaps two, of the four walls of the stockade was a range of cabins—or rather, one long cabin with log partitions—with the slope of the roof turned inward to the square; this furnished a platform for the garrison, who, protected by the rampart of pointed logs, could fire into the attacking party. Other platforms were bracketed against the walls not backed by cabins. There was a large double gate made of thick slabs and so situated as to be guarded by the blockhouses on either corner; this was the main entrance, but another and smaller gate furnished a rear exit to and entrance from the spring hard by. Blockhouses, cabins, and walls were all amply provided with port-holes; Fort Dobbs had capacity for a hundred men-at-arms to fire at one volley. Destructive fusillades could be maintained from within, and everywhere the walls were bullet-proof; but good marksmen in the attacking force could work great havoc by firing through the port-holes, and thus quietly picking off those who chanced to be in range. Fortunately for the whites few Indians became so expert as this.

Upon the arrival of breathless messengers bringing news of the approach of hostile Indians, the men, women, and children of a wide district would flock into such a fort as this. "I well remember," says Dr. Doddridge in his Notes on Virginia, "that when a little boy the family were sometimes waked up in the dead of night by an express with a report that the Indians were at hand. The express came softly to the door or back window, and by gentle tapping waked the family; this was easily done, as an habitual fear made us ever watchful and sensible to the slightest alarm. The whole family were instantly in motion: my father seized his gun and other implements of war; my stepmother waked up and dressed the children as well as she could; and being myself the oldest of the children, I had to take my share of the burthens to be carried to the fort. There was no possibility of getting a horse in the night to aid us in removing to the fort; besides the little children, we caught up what articles of clothing and provisions we could get hold of in the dark, for we durst not light a candle or even stir the fire. All this was done with the utmost despatch and the silence of death; the greatest care was taken not to awaken the youngest child; to the rest it was enough to say *Indian*, and not a whimper was heard afterwards. Thus it often happened that the whole number of families belonging to a fort, who were in the evening at their homes, were all in their little fortress before the dawn of the next morning. In the course of the succeeding day their household furniture was brought in by parties of the men under arms."

The large public frontier forts, such as we have described, did not house all of the backwoodsmen. There were some who, either because of great distance or other reasons, erected their own private defenses; or, in many cases, several isolated families united in such a structure. Often these were but single blockhouses, with a few outlying cabins. It was difficult to induce some of the more venturesome folk to enter the forts unless Indians were actually in the settlement; they took great risks in order to care for their crops and stock until the last moment; and, soon tiring of the monotony of life within the fort cabins, would often leave the refuge before the danger was really over. "Such families," reports Doddridge, "gave no small amount of trouble by creating frequent necessities of sending runners to warn them of their danger, and sometimes parties of our men to protect them during their removal."

For the first few years Fort Dobbs was but little used. There was, however, much uneasiness. The year 1757 had, all along the line, been disastrous to English arms in the North, and the Cherokees became increasingly insolent. The next year they committed several deadly assaults in the Valley of Virginia, but themselves suffered greatly in return. The French, at last driven from Fort Duquesne (Pittsburg), had retreated down the Ohio River to Fort Massac, in southern Illinois, and sent their emissaries far and near to stir up the Indians west of the mountains. The following April (1759) the Yadkin and Catawba Valleys were raided by the Cherokees, with the usual results of ruined crops, burned farm-buildings, and murdered households; not a few of the borderers being carried off as prisoners into the Indian country, there generally to suffer either slavery or slow death from the most horrid forms of torture. The Catawbas, meanwhile, remained faithful to their white friends.

Until this outbreak the Carolinas had prospered greatly. Hundreds of settlers had poured in from the more exposed northern valleys, and the western uplands were now rapidly being dotted over with clearings and log cabins. The Indian forays at once created a general panic throughout this region, heretofore considered safe. Most of the Yadkin families, together with English fur-traders who hurried in from the woods, huddled within the walls either of Fort Dobbs or of small neighborhood forts hastily constructed; but many others, in their fright, fled with all their possessions to settlements on or near the Atlantic coast.

Among the latter were old Squire Boone and his wife, Daniel and Rebecca, with their two sons,* and several other families of Bryans and Boones, although some of both names preferred to remain at Fort Dobbs. The fugitives scattered to various parts of Virginia and Maryland—Squire going to Georgetown, now in the District of Columbia, where he lived for three years and then returned to the Yadkin; while Daniel's family went in their two-horse wagon to Culpeper County, in eastern Virginia. The settlers there employed him with his wagon in hauling tobacco to Fredericksburg, the nearest market-town.

The April forays created almost as much consternation at Charleston as on the Yadkin. Governor Lyttleton, of South Carolina, sent out fifteen hundred men to overcome the

---

* The children of Daniel Boone were as follows: James (born in 1757), Israel (1759), Susannah (1760), Jemima (1762), Lavinia (1766), Rebecca (1768), Daniel Morgan (1769), John B. (1773), and Nathan (1780). The four daughters all married and died in Kentucky. The two eldest sons were killed by Indians, the three younger emigrated to Missouri.

Cherokees, who now pretended to be grieved at the acts of their young hot-bloods and patched up a peace. Fur-traders, eager to renew their profitable barter, hastened back into the western forests. But very soon their confidence was shattered, for the Indians again dug up the tomahawk. Their war-parties infested every road and trail; most of the traders, with trains of packhorses to carry their goods and furs, fell an easy prey to their forest customers; and Forts Loudon, Dobbs, and Prince George were besieged. By January (1760) the entire southwest border was once more a scene of carnage.

Captain Waddell, our old friend of Braddock's campaign, commanded at Fort Dobbs, with several Bryans and Boones in his little garrison. Here the Cherokees were repulsed with great loss. At Fort Prince George the country round about was sadly harried by the enemy, who finally withdrew. Fort Loudon, however, had one of the saddest experiences in the thrilling annals of the frontier.

In April General Amherst, of the British Army, sent Colonel Montgomery against the

Cherokees with a formidable column composed of twelve hundred regular troops—among them six hundred kilted Highlanders—to whom were attached seven hundred Carolina backwoods rangers under Waddell, with some Catawba allies. They laid waste with fire and sword all the Cherokee villages on the Keowee and Tennessee Rivers, including the growing crops and magazines of corn. The soldiers killed seventy Indians, captured forty prisoners, and reduced the greater part of the tribe to the verge of starvation.

The Cherokees were good fighters, and soon had their revenge. On the morning of the twenty-seventh of June the army was proceeding along a rough road on the southern bank of the Little Tennessee, where on one side is a sheer descent to the stream, on the other a lofty cliff. Here it was ambuscaded by over six hundred savage warriors under the noted chief Silouee. In the course of an engagement lasting several hours the whites lost twenty killed and sixty wounded, and the Cherokee casualties were perhaps greater. Montgomery desperately beat his way to a level tract, but in the night hastily withdrew, and did not stop until he reached Charleston. Despite the entreaties of the Assembly, he at once retired to the North with his little army, and left the frontiers of Carolina open to the assaults of the merciless foe.

The siege of Fort Loudon was now pushed by the Cherokees with vigor. It had already withstood several desperate and protracted assaults. But the garrison contrived to exist for several months, almost wholly upon the active sympathy of several Indian women who were married to frontiersmen shut up within the walls. The dusky wives frequently contrived to smuggle food into the fort despite the protests of the Indian leaders. Women, however, despite popular notions to the contrary, have a powerful influence in Indian camps; and they but laughed the chiefs to scorn, saying that they would suffer death rather than refuse assistance to their white husbands.

This relief, however, furnished but a precarious existence. Receiving no help from the settlements, which were cut off from communication with them, and weak from irregular food, the garrison finally surrendered on promise of a safe-conduct to their fellows in the East. Early in the morning of August ninth they marched out—men, women, and children to the number of several hundred—leaving behind them their cannon, ammunition, and spare arms. The next day, upon their sorry march, they were set upon by a bloodthirsty mob of seven hundred Cherokees. Many were killed outright, others surrendered merely to meet torture and death. Finally, after several hours of horror, a friendly chief succeeded, by browbeating his people and by subterfuge, in saving the lives of about two hundred persons, who in due time and after great suffering, reached the relief party which had for several months been making its way thither from Virginia; but it had been delayed by storms and high water in the mountain streams, and was now seeking needed rest in a camp at the head of the Holston. It is recorded that during the heartrending mêlée several other Indians risked their lives for white friends, performing deeds of heroism which deserve to be remembered.

Although New France was now tottering to its fall, the French officers at Fort Massac still continued, with their limited resources, to keep alive the Cherokee war spirit. French outrages occurred throughout the autumn and early winter of 1760. At nearly all of the forts, large and small, skirmishes took place, some of these giving occasion for exhibitions of rare enterprise and courage on the part of the garrisons, women and men alike.

During the winter, the governors of Virginia, North Carolina, and South Carolina agreed upon a joint campaign against the hostiles. The southern column, comprising twenty-six hundred men, chiefly Highlanders, was under Lieutenant-Colonel James Grant. Starting early in June, they carried with them seven hundred packhorses, four hundred head of cattle, and a large train of baggage and supplies. Their route from Fort Prince George to the lower and middle Cherokee towns on the Little Tennessee lay through a rough, mountainous country; high water, storms, intensely warm weather, the lack of tents, and bruises from rocks and briers, caused the troops to suffer greatly. After heavy losses from ambuscades in narrow defiles, they finally reached their destination, and spent a month in burning and ravaging fifteen or more large villages and fourteen hundred acres of growing corn, and in driving five thousand men, women, and children into the hills to starve. Wrote one of the pious participators in this terrible work of devastation: "Heaven has blest us with the greatest success; we have finished our business as completely as the most sanguine of us could have wished." The Cherokees, completely crushed, humbly begged for peace, which was granted upon liberal terms and proved to be permanent.

The northern column was composed of backwoodsmen from Virginia and North Carolina, under Colonel William Byrd, an experienced campaigner. Byrd was much hampered for both men and supplies, and accomplished little. He appears to have largely spent his time in making roads and building blockhouses—laborious methods ill-fitted for Indian warfare, and loudly criticized by Waddell, who joined him with a regiment of five hundred North Carolinians, among whom was Daniel Boone, now returned to the Yadkin. Waddell and Boone had experienced the folly of this sort of thing in Braddock's ill-fated campaign. As a result of dissatisfaction, Byrd resigned, and Colonel Stephen succeeded him. The force, now composed of about twelve hundred men, pushed on to the Long Island of Holston River, where they were met by four hundred Cherokees, who, brought to their knees by Grant, likewise sought peace from Stephen. Articles were accordingly signed on the nineteenth of November. The North Carolina men returned home; but a portion of the Virginia regiment remained as a winter garrison for Fort Robinson, as the new fort at Long Island was called.

Now that the Yadkin region has, after its sad experience, been blessed with a promise of peace, we may well pause, briefly to consider the ethics of border warfare. This life-history will, to its close, have much to do with Indian forays and white reprisals, and it is well that we should consider them dispassionately.

Red Man Against White Man

The Cherokees were conducting a warfare in defense of their villages, fields, and hunting-grounds, which were being rapidly destroyed by the inrush of white settlers, who seemed to think that the Indians had no rights worth consideration. Encouraged by the French, who deemed the English intruders on lands which they had first explored, the American aborigines seriously thought that they might stem the tide of English settlement. It was impossible that they should win, for civilization has in such cases ever triumphed over savagery; but that they should make the attempt was to be expected from a high-spirited race trained to war. We can but sympathize with and honor them for making their several stout stands against the European wave which was ultimately to sweep them from their native land.* King

---

* "I had rather receive the blessing of one poor Cherokee, as he casts his last look back upon his country, for having, though in vain, attempted to prevent his banishment, than to sleep beneath the marble of all the Cæsars."—*Extract from a speech of Theodore Frelinghuysen, of New Jersey, delivered in the United States Senate, April 7, 1830.*

"I am not aware that any community has a right to force another to be civilized."—*John Stuart Mill.*

Philip, Opecancano, Pontiac, Tecumseh, Red Jacket, Sitting Bull, Captain Jack, were types of successive leaders who, at various stages of our growth westward, have stood as bravely as any Spartan hero to contest our all-conquering advance.

It is the time-honored custom of historians of the frontier to consider Indians as all wrong and whites as all right; and that, of course, was the opinion of the borderers themselves—of Daniel Boone and all the men of his day. But we are now far enough removed from these events, and the fierce passions they engendered, to see them more clearly. The Indian was a savage and fought like a savage—cruel, bloodthirsty, unrelenting, treacherous, seldom a respecter of childhood, of age, or of women. But one can not read closely the chronicles of border warfare without discovering that civilized men at times could, in fighting savages, descend quite as low in the scale as they, in bloodthirstiness and treachery. Some of the most atrocious acts in the pioneer history of Kentucky and the Middle West were performed by whites; and some of the most

Christianlike deeds—there were many such on both sides—were those of painted savages.

It is needless to blame either of the contending races; their conflict was inevitable. The frontiersman was generally unlettered, and used, without ceremony, to overcoming the obstacles which nature set in his path; one more patient could not have tamed the wilderness as quickly as he. His children often rose to high positions as scholars, statesmen, and diplomats. But he himself was a diamond in the rough, and not accustomed to nice ethical distinctions. To his mind the Indian was an inferior being, if not a child of Satan; he was not making the best use of the soil; his customs and habits of thought were such as to repel the British mind, however much they may have attracted the French. The tribesmen, whom the pioneer could not and would not understand, stood in his way, hence must be made to go or to die in his tracks. When the savage, quick to resentment, struck back, the turbulent passions of the overbearing white were aroused, and with compound interest he repaid the blow. Upon the theory that the devil must be fought with fire, the borderer not seldom adopted methods of reprisal that outdid the savage in brutality.

The red man fighting, after his own wild standards, for all that he held most dear, and the white man, who brooks no opposition from an inferior race, hitting back with a fury sometimes increased by fear—such, in brief, is the blood-stained history of the American border.

CHAPTER V.

KENTUCKY REACHED AT LAST

WHEN Daniel Boone returned from tidewater Virginia to the Yadkin region is not now known. It is probable that the monotony of hauling tobacco to market at a time when his old neighbors were living in a state of panic palled upon a man who loved excitement and had had a taste of Indian warfare. It has been surmised that he served with the Rowan rangers upon Lyttleton's campaign, alluded to in the previous chapter, and possibly aided in defending Fort Dobbs, or served with Waddell under Montgomery. That he was, some time in 1760, in the mountains west of the Yadkin upon either a hunt or a scout, or both, appears to be well established; for up to a few years ago there was still standing upon the banks of Boone's Creek, a small tributary of the Watauga in eastern Tennessee, a tree upon whose smooth bark had been rudely carved this characteristic legend, undoubtedly by the great hunter himself: " D Boon cilled A BAR on this tree year 1760." *

We have already seen that he accompanied Waddell in 1761, when that popular frontier leader reenforced Colonel Byrd's expedition against the Cherokees. Upon Waddell's return to North Carolina his leather-shirted followers dispersed to their homes, and Boone was again enabled to undertake a protracted hunt, no longer disturbed by fear that in his absence Indians might raid the settlement; for hunting was now his chief occupation, his wife and children conducting the farm, which held second place in his affections. Thus we see how close the borderers came to the savage life wherein men are the warriors and hunters and women the crop-gatherers and housekeepers. Organizing a party of kindred spirits—a goodly portion of the Yadkin settlers were more hunters than farmers—Boone crossed the mountains and roamed through the valleys of southwest

* Boone had a strong fancy for carving his name and hunting feats upon trees. His wanderings have very largely been traced by this means.

A BOONE TREE.

Tree on Boone's Creek, Tenn., bearing Daniel Boone's autograph.
(See pp. 55, 56.)

Virginia and eastern Tennessee, being especially delighted with the Valley of the Holston, where game was found to be unusually abundant. At about the same time another party of nineteen hunters went upon a similar expedition into the hills and valleys westward of the Yadkin, penetrating well into Tennessee, and being absent for eighteen months.

We must not conclude, from the passionate devotion to hunting exhibited by these backwoodsmen of the eighteenth century, that they led the same shiftless, aimless lives as are followed by the "poor whites" found in some of the river-bottom communities of our own day, who are in turn farmers, fishermen, or hunters, as fancy or the seasons dictate. It must be remembered that farming upon the Virginia and Carolina uplands was, in the pioneer period, crude as to methods and insignificant as to crops. The principal wealth of the well-to-do was in herds of horses and cattle which grazed in wild meadows, and in droves of long-nosed swine feeding upon the roots and acorns of the hillside forests. Among the outlying settlers much of the family food came from the woods, and often months would pass without bread being seen inside the cabin walls. Besides the live stock of the richer folk, whose herds were driven to market, annual caravans to tide-water towns carried furs and skins won by the real backwoodsmen, who lived on the fringe of the wilderness. For lack of money accounts were kept in pelts, and with these were purchased rifles, ammunition, iron, and salt. It was, then, to the forests that the borderers largely looked for their sustenance. Hence those long hunts, from which the men of the Yadkin, unerring marksmen, would come back laden with great packs of pelts for the markets, and dried venison, bear's meat, and bear's oil for their family larders. Naturally, this wandering, adventurous life, spiced with excitement in many forms, strongly appealed to the rough, hardy borderers, and unfitted them for other occupations. Under such conditions farming methods were not likely to improve, nor the arts of civilization to prosper; for the hunter not only best loved the wilderness, but settlement narrowed his hunting-grounds. Thus it was that the frontiersman of the Daniel Boone type, Indian hater as he was, had at heart much the same interests as the savage whom he was seeking to supplant. It was simply a question as to which hunter, red or white, should occupy the forest; to neither was settlement welcome.

With the opening of 1762 the southwest border began to be reoccupied. The abandoned log cabins once more had fires lighted upon their hearths, at the base of the great outside chimneys of stones and mud-plastered boughs; the deserted clearings, which had become choked with weeds and underbrush in the five years of Indian warfare, were again cultivated by their reassured owners. Among the returned refugees were Daniel's parents, Squire and Sarah Boone, who had ridden on horseback overland all the way from Maryland. Three years later Squire Boone died, one of the most highly esteemed men in the valley.

The Yadkin country was more favored than some other portions of the backwoods of North Carolina. Pontiac's uprising (1763) against the English, who had now supplanted the French in Canada and in the wilderness between the Alleghanies and the Mississippi, led some of the Southern tribes again to attack the frontiers of the Southwest; but they were defeated before the Yadkin was affected by this fresh panic.

The Indian wars had lasted so long that the entire border had become demoralized. Of course not all the people in the backwoods were of good character. Not a few of them had been driven out from the more thickly settled parts of the country because of crimes or of bad reputation; and some of the fur-traders who lived upon the edge of the settlement were sorry rogues. When the panic-stricken people were crowded within the narrow walls of the forts they could not work. Many of them found this life of enforced idleness to their liking, and fell into the habit of making secret expeditions to plunder abandoned houses and to steal uncared-for live stock. When peace came these marauders had acquired a distaste for honest labor; leaving the forts, they pillaged right and left, and horse-stealing became an especially prevalent frontier vice.

Justice on the border was as yet insufficiently organized. Some of the Virginia and Carolina magistrates were themselves rascals, whose decisions could be purchased by criminals. Many of the best citizens, therefore, formed associations whose members were called "regulators." They bound themselves to pursue, arrest, and try criminals, and to punish them by whipping, also by expulsion from the neighborhood. The law-breakers, on the other hand, organized in defense, and popular opinion was divided between the two elements; for there were some good people who did not like the arbitrary methods of the regulators, and insisted upon every man being given a regular trial by jury. In South Carolina, particularly, the settlers were much exercised on this question, and arrayed themselves into opposing bands, armed to carry out their respective views. For a time civil war was feared; but finally, after five years of disturbance, an agreement was reached, efficient courts were established, and justice triumphed.

Affairs did not reach so serious a stage in North Carolina. Nevertheless there were several bands of vicious and indolent men, who, entrenched in the hills, long defied the regulators. One of these parties built a rude stockaded fort beneath an overhanging cliff in the mountains back of the Yadkin settlements. They stole horses, cattle, farming utensils; in fact, anything that they could lay their hands upon. One day they grew so bold as to kidnap a girl. The settlers, now roused to action, organized attacking companies, one of them headed by Daniel Boone, and carried the log fortress of the bandits by storm. The culprits were taken to Salisbury jail and the clan broken up.

The rapid growth of the country soon made game scarce in Boone's neighborhood. Not only did the ever-widening area of cleared fields destroy the cover, but there were, of course, more hunters than before. Thus our Nimrod, who in his early manhood cared for nothing smaller than deer, was compelled to take extended trips in his search for less-frequented places. It was not long before he had explored all the mountains and valleys within easy reach, and become familiar with the views from every peak in the region, many of them five and six thousand feet in height.

As early as 1764–65 Boone was in the habit of taking with him, upon these trips near home, his little son James, then seven or eight years of age. This was partly for company, but mainly for the lad's education as a hunter. Frequently they would spend several days together in the woods during the autumn and early winter—the deer-hunting season—and often, when in "open" camps, were overtaken by snow-storms. On such occasions the father would keep the boy warm by clasping him to his bosom as they lay with feet toward the glowing camp-fire. As the well-taught lad grew into early manhood these two companions would be absent from home for two and three months together, always returning well laden with the spoils of the chase.

Hunters in Boone's day had two kinds of camp—"open" when upon the move, which meant sleeping in their blankets upon the ground wherever darkness or weariness overtook them; "closed" where remaining for some time in a locality. A closed camp consisted of a rude hut of logs or poles, the front entirely open, the sides closely chinked with moss, and the roof covered with blankets, boughs, or bark, sloping down to a back-log. In times when the Indians were not feared a fire was kept up throughout the night, in front, in order to warm the enclosure. Upon a bed of hemlock boughs or of dried leaves the hunters lay with heads to the back-log and stockinged feet to the blaze, for their spongy moccasins were hung to dry.* Such a camp, often called a "half-faced cabin," was carefully placed so that it might be sheltered by neighboring hills from the cold north and west winds. It was fairly successful as a protection from rain and snow, and sometimes served a party of hunters throughout several successive seasons; but it was ill-fitted for the coldest weather. Boone frequently occupied a shelter of this kind in the woods of Kentucky.

During the last four months of 1765 Boone and seven companions went on horseback to the new colony of Florida with a view

---

* When Indians were about, moccasins were always tied to the guns so as to be ready to slip on in case of a night alarm.

to moving thither if they found it suited to their tastes. Wherever possible, they stopped overnight at borderers' cabins upon the frontiers of the Carolinas and Georgia. But such opportunities did not always occur; they often suffered from hunger, and once they might have died from starvation but for the timely succor of a roving band of Seminole Indians. They explored Florida all the way from St. Augustine to Pensacola, and appear to have had a rather wretched time of it. The trails were miry from frequent rains, the number and extent of the swamps appalled them, and there was not game enough to satisfy a man like Boone, who scorned alligators. Pensacola, however, so pleased him that he determined to settle there, and purchased a house and lot which he might in due time occupy. Upon their return Boone told his wife of his Pensacola venture, but this sturdy woman of the frontier spurned the idea of moving to a gameless land. So the town lot was left to take care of itself, and henceforth the dutiful husband looked only to the West as his model of a perfect country.

Daniel Boone

At the close of the French and Indian War there arrived in the Boone settlement a Scotch-Irishman named Benjamin Cutbirth, aged about twenty-three years. He was a man of good character and a fine hunter. Marrying Elizabeth Wilcoxen, a niece of Daniel Boone, he and Boone went upon long hunts together, and attained that degree of comradeship which joint life in a wilderness camp is almost certain to produce.

In 1766 several families from North Carolina went to Louisiana, apparently by sea to New Orleans, and founded an English settlement above Baton Rouge on the Mississippi River. The news of this event gave rise to a general desire for exploring the country between the mountains and the great river. The year following, Cutbirth, John Stuart, John Baker, and John Ward, all of them young married men on the Yadkin, and excellent hunters, resolved to perform this feat, and if possible to discover a region superior to their own valley. They crossed the mountain range and eventually saw the Mississippi, being, so far as we know from contemporary documents, the first party of white men to succeed in this overland enterprise. Possibly fur-traders may have done so before them, but they left no record to prove it.

Cutbirth and his friends spent a year or two upon the river. In the autumn they ascended the stream for a considerable distance, also one of its tributaries, made a stationary camp for the winter, and in the spring descended to New Orleans, where they sold at good prices their skins, furs, bear-bacon, bear's oil, buffalo "jerk" (dried meat), tallow, and dried venison hams. Their expedition down the river was performed at great risks, for they had many hairbreadth escapes from snags, river banks shelving in, whirlpools, wind-storms, and Indians. Their reward, says a chronicler of the day, was "quite a respectable property;" but while upon their return homeward, overland, they were set upon by Choctaws, who robbed them of their all.

Meanwhile, Daniel Boone was slow in making up his mind to leave home and the wife and family whom he dearly loved for so long and perilous a trip as a journey into the now much-talked-of land of Kentucky. Perhaps, despite his longings, he might never have gone had affairs upon the Yadkin remained satisfactory to him. But game, his chief reliance, was year by year becoming harder to obtain. And the rascally agents of Earl Granville, the principal landholder of the region, from whom the Boones had purchased, were pretending to find flaws in the land-titles and insisting upon the necessity for new deeds, for which large fees were exacted.

This gave rise to great popular discontent. Boone's protest consisted in leaving the Sugar Tree settlement and moving northwest for sixty-five miles toward the head of the Yadkin. His new cabin, a primitive shell of logs, could still be seen, a few years ago, at the foot of a range of hills some seven and a half miles above Wilkesboro, in Wilkes County. After a time, dissatisfied with this location, he moved five miles farther up the river and about half a mile up Beaver Creek. Again he changed his mind, choosing his final home on the upper Yadkin, just above the mouth of Beaver. It was from this beautiful region among the Alleghany foot-hills, where game and fish were plenty and his swine and cattle had good range, that Boone, crowded out by advancing civilization, eventually moved to Kentucky.

In the spring and early summer of 1767 there were fresh outbreaks on the part of the Indians. Governor Tryon had run a boundary-line between the back settlements of the Carolinas and the Cherokee hunting-grounds. But hunters and traders would persist in wandering to the west of this line, and sometimes they were killed.

In the autumn of that year Daniel Boone and a warm friend, William Hill, and possibly Squire Boone, determined to seek Kentucky, of which Finley had told him twelve years before. They crossed the mountain wall, were in the valleys of the Holston and the Clinch, and reached the head waters of the West Fork of the Big Sandy. Following down this river for a hundred miles, determined to find the Ohio, they appear to have struck a buffalo-path, along which they traveled as far as a salt-lick ten miles west of the present town of Prestonburg, on a tributary of the West (or Louisa) Fork of the Sandy, within Floyd County, in the extreme eastern part of Kentucky.

Caught in a severe snow-storm, they were compelled to camp at this lick for the entire winter. It proved to be the most profitable station that they could have selected, for buffaloes and other animals came in large numbers to lick the brackish soil, and all the hunters had to do was to " rise, kill, and eat."

Although now considerably west of the Cumberland Mountains, the explorers were not aware that they were within the famed Kentucky; and as the country was very hilly, covered with briers which annoyed them greatly, and altogether forbidding, they despaired of reaching the promised land by this path, and in the spring returned to the Yadkin.

CHAPTER VI

ALONE IN THE WILDERNESS

In the winter of 1768–69 a pedler with horse and wagon wandered into the valley of the upper Yadkin, offering small wares to the settlers' wives. This was thrifty John Finley, former fur-trader and Indian fighter, who, thirteen years before, had, as we have seen, fraternized with Boone in Braddock's ill-fated army on the Monongahela. Finley had, in 1752, in his trade with the Indians, descended the Ohio in a canoe to the site of Louisville, accompanied by three or four voyageurs, and, with some of his dusky customers, traveled widely through the interior of Kentucky. His glowing descriptions of this beautiful land had inspired Boone to try to find it. The latter was still sorrowing over his unpromising expedition by way of the Big Sandy when, by the merest chance, the man who had fired his imagination knocked at his very door.

Throughout the winter that Finley was Daniel's guest, he and his brother Squire were ready listeners to the pedler's stories of the over-mountain country—tales of countless water-fowl, turkeys, deer, elk, and buffaloes, which doubtless lost nothing in the telling. The two Boones resolved to try Finley's proposed route by way of Cumberland Gap, and the fur-trader promised to lead the way.

After the spring crops were in, Finley, Daniel Boone, and the latter's brother-in-law, John Stuart, started from Daniel's house upon the first of May. In their employ, as hunters and camp-keepers, were three neighbors—Joseph Holden, James Mooney, and William Cooley. Each man was fully armed, clad in the usual deerskin costume of the frontier, and mounted upon a good horse; blanket or bearskin was strapped on behind the saddle, together with camp-kettle, a store of salt, and a small supply of provisions, although their chief food was to be game. Squire remained to care for the crops of the two families, and agreed to reenforce the hunters late in the autumn.

Scaling the lofty Blue Ridge, the explorers

passed over Stone and Iron Mountains and reached Holston Valley, whence they proceeded through Moccasin Gap of Clinch Mountain, and crossed over intervening rivers and densely wooded hills until they came to Powell's Valley, then the farthest limit of white settlement. Here they found a hunter's trail which led them through Cumberland Gap. The "warriors' path"—trodden by Indian war-parties from across the mountains—was now discovered, and this they followed by easy stages until at last they reached what is now called Station Camp Creek, a tributary of the Kentucky River, in Estill County, Ky.—so named because here was built their principal, or "station" camp, the center of their operations for many months to come.

While Boone, Finley, and Stuart made frequent explorations, and Boone in particular ascended numerous lofty hills in order to view the country, the chief occupation of the party was hunting. Throughout the summer and autumn deerskins were in their best condition. Other animals were occasionally killed to afford variety of food, but fur-bearers as a rule only furnish fine pelts in the winter season. Even in the days of abundant game the hunter was required to exercise much skill, patience, and endurance. It was no holiday task to follow this calling. Deer, especially, were difficult to obtain. The habits of this excessively cautious animal were carefully studied; the hunter must know how to imitate its various calls, to take advantage of wind and weather, and to practise all the arts of strategy.

Deerskins were, all things considered, the most remunerative of all. When roughly dressed and dried they were worth about a dollar each; as they were numerous, and a horse could carry for a long distance about a hundred such skins, the trade was considered profitable in those primitive times, when dollars were hard to obtain. Pelts of beavers, found in good condition only in the winter, were worth about two dollars and a half each, and of otters from three to five dollars. Thus, a horse-load of beaver furs, when obtainable, was worth about five times that of a load of deerskins; and if a few otters could be thrown in, the value was still greater. The skins of buffaloes, bears, and elks were too bulky to carry for long distances, and were not readily marketable. A few elk-hides were needed, however, to cut up into harness and straps, and bear- and buffalo-robes were useful for bedding.

When an animal was killed the hunter skinned it on the spot, and packed on his back the hide and the best portion of the meat. At night the meat was smoked or prepared for "jerking," and the skins were scraped and cured. When collected at the camps, the bales of skins, protected from the weather by strips of bark, were placed upon high scaffolds, secure from bears and wolves.

Our Yadkin hunters were in the habit, each day, of dividing themselves into pairs for company and mutual aid in times of danger, usually leaving one pair behind as camp-keepers. Boone and Stuart frequently were companions upon such trips; for the former, being a man of few words, enjoyed by contrast the talkative, happy disposition of his friend. Occasionally the entire party, when the game grew timid, moved for some distance, where they would establish a new camp; but their headquarters remained at Station Camp, where were kept their principal skins, furs, and stores. In this way the time passed from June to December. Boone used to assert, in after years, that these months were the happiest of his life. The genial climate, the beauty of the country, and the entire freedom of this wild life, strongly appealed to him. Here this taciturn but good-natured man, who loved solitary adventure, was now in his element. Large packs of skins had been obtained by the little company and stored at Station Camp and their outlying shelters; and there was now a generous supply of buffalo, bear, and elk meat, venison, and turkeys, all properly jerked for the winter which was before them, with buffalo tallow and bear's oil to serve as cooking grease.

Finley and Boone were both aware that Kentucky lay between the warring tribes of the North and the South; that through it warriors' paths crossed in several directions; and that this, probably the finest hunting-field in North America, was a debatable land, frequently fought over by contending savages—a "dark and bloody ground" indeed. Yet thus far there had been no signs of Indians, and the Carolina hunters had almost ceased to think of them.

Toward the close of day on the twenty-second of December, while Boone and Stuart were ascending a low hill near the Kentucky River, in one of the most beautiful districts they had seen, they were suddenly surrounded and captured by a large party of Shawnese horsemen returning from an autumn hunt on Green River to their homes north of the Ohio. The two captives were forced to lead the savages to their camps, which were deliberately plundered, one after the other, of everything in them. The Shawnese, releasing their prisoners, considerately left with each hunter just enough supplies to enable him to support himself on the way back to the settlements. The white men were told what was a fact under existing treaties with the tribes—treaties, however, of which Boone and his companions probably knew nothing—that they were trespassing upon Indian hunting-grounds, and must not come again, or "the wasps and yellow-jackets will sting you severely."

The others proposed to leave for home at once; but Boone and Stuart, enraged at having lost their year's work and all that they had brought into the wilderness, and having no sympathy for Indian treaty rights, started out to recover their property. After two days they came up with the Shawnese, and secreting themselves in the bushes until dark, contrived to regain four or five horses and make off with them. But they, in turn, were overtaken in two days by the Indians and again made prisoners. After a week of captivity, in which they were kindly treated, they effected their escape in the dark and returned to Station Camp.

Their companions, giving them up for lost, had departed toward home, but were overtaken by the two adventurers. Boone was gratified to find with them his brother Squire, who, having gathered the fall crops, had come out with a fresh supply of horses, traps, and ammunition. He had followed the trail of his predecessors, and in the New River region was joined by Alexander Neely.

Not finding Daniel and Stuart at Station Camp, and grief-stricken at the report concerning them, he was traveling homeward with the party.

Daniel, however, who had staked upon this venture almost all that he owned, did not relish the thought of returning empty-handed, now that reenforcements had arrived, and determined to stay and seek to regain his lost fortunes. Squire, Stuart, and Neely concluded also to remain, and the four were now left behind in the wilderness. On reaching the Holston Valley, Finley turned northward to seek his relatives in Pennsylvania; while Holden, Mooney, and Cooley proceeded southeastward to their Yadkin homes, carrying dismal news of the events attending this notable exploration of Kentucky.

The quartette promptly abandoned Station Camp as being dangerously near the warriors' path, and, tradition says, built another on or near the northern bank of Kentucky River, not far from the mouth of the Red. The deer season was now over, but beavers and otters were in their prime, and soon the hunters were enjoying a profitable season. A small canoe which they built added greatly to their equipment, and they were now enabled to set their traps throughout a wide region.

Hunting in pairs, Daniel was generally accompanied by Stuart, while Neely and Squire were partners. In their wanderings the two pairs were sometimes several days without seeing each other; and frequently partners would be separated throughout the day, but at night met at some appointed spot. One day, toward the close of January or early in February (1770), Stuart did not return to the rendezvous, much to Boone's alarm. The following day the latter discovered the embers of a fire, doubtless built by the lost man; but that was all, for Stuart was seen no more. Five years later Boone came across the bones of his light-hearted comrade in a hollow sycamore tree upon Rockcastle River—he recognized them by Stuart's name cut upon his powder-horn. What caused Stuart's death is a mystery to the present day; possibly he was wounded and chased by Indians to this distant spot, and died while in hiding.

Alone in the Wilderness

Stuart's mysterious disappearance frightened Neely, who at once left for home, thus leaving Daniel and Squire to pass the remainder of the winter in the wilderness by themselves. Dejected, but not discouraged, the brothers built a comfortable hut and continued their work. With the close of the trapping season the ammunition was nearly exhausted. Upon the first of May, a year after Daniel had left his cabin upon the upper Yadkin, Squire started out upon the return, their horses well laden with furs, skins, and jerked meat. Both men had, in their enterprise, contracted debts of considerable extent for frontier hunters, hence they were anxious to square themselves with the world, as well as to obtain more horses, ammunition, and miscellaneous supplies.

Daniel was now left alone in Kentucky, "without bread, salt, or sugar, without company of his fellow-creatures, or even a horse or dog." In after years he acknowledged that he was at times homesick during the three months which followed, and felt deeply his absence from the wife and family to whom he was so warmly attached. But possessing a cheerful, hopeful nature, he forgot his loneliness in untrammeled enjoyment of the far-stretching wilderness.

Almost without ammunition, he could not hunt, save to obtain sufficient food, and largely spent his time in exploration. Fearing Indians, he frequently changed his location, sometimes living in shelters of bark and boughs, and again in caves; but seldom venturing to sleep in these temporary homes, preferring the thickets and the dense canebrakes as less liable to be sought by savage prowlers.

Kentucky has a remarkably diversified landscape of densely wooded hills and valleys and broad prairie expanses. The genial climate admirably suited the philosophical wanderer. He enjoyed the exquisite beauty and stateliness of the trees—the sycamores, tulip-trees, sugar-trees, honey-locusts, coffee-trees, pawpaws, cucumber-trees, and black mulberries—and found flowers in surprising variety and loveliness. The mineral springs interested him—Big Lick, the Blue Licks, and Big Bone Lick, with its fossil remains of mastodons which had become mired when coming to lick the brackish soil. He traveled far and wide in his search for the beautiful and curious, being chiefly in the valleys of the Licking and the Kentucky, and upon the banks of the Ohio as far down as the site of Louisville, where, at the foot of the falls, he inspected the remains of an old fur trade stockade concerning which Finley had told him.

Once he saw some Indians walking upon the northern bank of the Ohio, but managed himself to keep out of sight. At another time, when on the Kentucky, he saw a savage calmly fishing from the trunk of a fallen tree. In mentioning this incident to his family, in later days, he would declare with gravity: "While I was looking at the fellow he tumbled into the river, and I saw him no more." Probably the man of the Yadkin shot him, fearing that the fisherman might carry the news of the former's whereabouts to a possible camp near by. On another occasion, when exploring Dick's River, he was suddenly surrounded by Indians. Having either to surrender or to leap down the precipitous height to a bank sixty feet below, he chose to leap. Landing in the top of a small sugar-maple, he slid down the tree, and was able to escape by running under the overhanging bank and then swimming the stream. Adventures such as this gave abundant spice to the joys of solitude.

In the latter part of July Squire arrived from the settlements, having paid all their debts and with the surplus purchased sufficient supplies for another summer and fall campaign against the deer. This was highly successful. They did not lack some interesting experiences, but Indians were not again encountered; so that, when winter approached, Squire was enabled once more to leave with well-laden horses for the markets of the East. Another two months of loneliness were suffered by Daniel; but in December Squire rejoined him with horses, ammunition, and other necessaries, and the pair joyously settled down for still another winter together in the dark and lonely forests of Kentucky.

CHAPTER VII

PREDECESSORS AND CONTEMPORARIES

THE reader of this narrative has, of course, already discovered that Daniel Boone was neither the original white explorer of Kentucky nor the first white hunter within its limits. Many others had been there before him. It will be worth our while at this point to take a hasty review of some of the previous expeditions which had made the "dark and bloody ground" known to the world.

Probably none of the several Spanish explorations of the sixteenth century along the Mississippi River and through the Gulf States had touched Kentucky. But during the seventeenth century both the French in Canada and the English on the Atlantic tidewater came to have fairly accurate notions of the country lying immediately to the south of the Ohio River. As early as 1650 Governor Berkeley, of Virginia, made a vain attempt to cross the Alleghany barrier in search of the Mississippi, concerning which he had heard from Indians; and we know that at the same time the French, especially the Jesuit missionaries, were looking eagerly in that direction. A few years later Colonel Abraham Wood, of Virginia, discovered streams which poured into the Ohio and the Mississippi. Just a century before Boone's great hunt, John Lederer, also of Virginia, explored for a considerable distance beyond the mountains. The following year Thomas Batts and his party proclaimed King Charles II upon New River, the upper waters of the Great Kanawha—twelve months before La Salle took possession of all Western waters for the French king, and nineteen before Marquette and Joliet discovered the Mississippi.

There is a tradition that in 1678, only five years after the voyage of Marquette and Joliet, a party of New Englanders ventured into the Western wilderness as far as New Mexico. The later French expeditions of La Salle, Hennepin, and D'Iberville are well known. Several Englishmen traded with Indians upon the Mississippi before the close of the seventeenth century; by 1719 the English were so numerous that Governor Keith, of Pennsylvania, suggested that four forts be built for their protection in the Wabash and Illinois countries. We hear of a French expedition investigating Big Bone Lick, in Kentucky, in 1735; and other visits were successively made by bands of their compatriots until the downfall of New France, over a quarter of a century later. In 1742 John Howard and Peter Salling, of Virginia, were exploring in Kentucky; six years after them Dr. Thomas Walker made a notable expedition through the same country; and two years after that Washington's backwoods friend, Christopher Gist, was on the site of Louisville selecting lands for the Ohio Company, which had a large grant upon the Ohio River.

Henceforward, border chronicles abound with reports of the adventures of English fur-traders, hunters, and land-viewers, all along the Ohio River and tributary waters above Louisville. Among these early adventurers was our friend Finley, whose experiences in Kentucky dated from 1752, and who piloted Boone to the promised land through the gateway of Cumberland Gap. The subsequent Indian wars, with the expeditions into the upper Ohio Valley by Generals Braddock, Forbes, and Bouquet, made the country still better known; and settlers were soon rushing in by scores, although as yet none of them appear to have made clearings within Kentucky itself.

Officers and soldiers who had served in the French and Indian War were given liberal grants of land in the West. Washington had not only his own grant, as the principal officer upon the southwest frontier, but was agent for a number of fellow-soldiers, and in 1767 went to the Ohio River to select and survey claims. At the very time when Boone was engaged upon his fruitless expedition down the Big Sandy, Washington was making the first surveys in Kentucky on both the Little and Big Sandy. Again, in 1770, when Boone was exploring the Kentucky wilderness, Washington was surveying extensive tracts along the Ohio and the Great Kanawha, and planning for a large colony upon his own lands. The outbreak of the Revolution caused the great man to turn his attention from the over-mountain region to the defense of his country. Had he been left to carry out his plans, he would doubtless have won fame as the most energetic of Western pioneers.

It will be remembered that when Boone and his companions passed through Cumberland Gap in the early summer of 1769, they found the well-worn trail of other hunters who had preceded them from the settlements. The men of the Yadkin Valley were not the only persons seeking game in Kentucky that year. At about the time when Boone was bidding farewell to his family, Hancock and Richard Taylor, Abraham Hempinstall, and one Barbour, frontiersmen of the same type, started from their homes in Orange County, Va., to explore the valleys of the Ohio and Mississippi. They descended from Pittsburg in a boat, explored Kentucky, and proceeded into Arkansas, where they camped and hunted during the following winter. The next year two of them traveled eastward to Florida, and thence northwardly to their homes; the others stayed in Arkansas for another year, and returned by sea from New Orleans to New York.

Simultaneously with the expeditions of Boone and the Taylors, a party of twenty or more adventurous hunters and explorers was formed in the New River region, in the Valley of Virginia. They set out in June (1769), piloted by Uriah Stone, who had been in Kentucky three years before. Entering by way of the now familiar Cumberland Gap, these men had experiences quite similar to those of Boone and his comrades. At some of the Kentucky salt-licks they found herds of buffaloes numbering up in the thousands —at one lick a hundred acres were densely massed with these bulky animals, who exhibited no fear until the wind blew from the hunters toward them, and then they would "dash wildly away in large droves and disappear." Like Boone's party, they also were the victims of Cherokees, who plundered their camps, and after leaving them some guns and a little ammunition, ordered them out of the country. The New River party being large, however, some of their number were deputed to go to the settlements and bring back fresh supplies, so that they could finish their hunt. After further adventures with Indians half of the hunters returned home; while the others wandered into Tennessee and as far as the Ozark Mountains, finally reaching New River through Georgia and the Carolinas. Another Virginian, named John McCulloch, who courted the perils of exploration, was in Kentucky in the summer of 1769 with a white man-servant and a negro. He visited the site of Terre Haute, Ind., and went by canoe to Natchez and New Orleans, and at length reached Philadelphia by sea.

But the most famous of all the expeditions of the period was that of the "Long Hunters," as they have come to be known in Western history. Inspired by the favorable reports of Stone and others, about forty of the most noted and successful hunters of New River and Holston Valleys formed, in the summer of 1770, a company for hunting and trapping to the west of Cumberland Mountains. Under the leadership of two of the best woodsmen of the region, Joseph

Drake and Henry Skaggs, and including several of Stone's party, they set out in early autumn fully prepared for meeting Indians and living on game. Each man took with him three packhorses, rifles, ammunition, traps, dogs, blankets, and salt, and was dressed in the deerskin costume of the times.

Pushing on through Cumberland Gap, the adventurers were soon in the heart of Kentucky. In accordance with custom, they visited some of the best licks—a few of which were probably first seen by them—for here wild beasts were always to be found in profusion. At Knob Licks they beheld from an eminence which overlooked the springs "what they estimated at largely over a thousand animals, including buffaloe, elk, bear, and deer, with many wild turkies scattered among them—all quite restless, some playing, and others busily employed in licking the earth; but at length they took flight and bounded away all in one direction, so that in the brief space of a couple of minutes not an animal was to be seen." Within an area of many acres, the animals had eaten the salty earth to a depth of several feet.

Successful in a high degree, the party ceased operations in February, and had completed preparations for sending a large shipment of skins, furs, and "jerk" to the settlements, when, in their temporary absence, roving Cherokees robbed them of much of their stores and spoiled the greater part of the remainder. "Fifteen hundred skins gone to ruination!" was the legend which one of them carved upon the bark of a neighboring tree, a record to which were appended the initials of each member of the party. A series of disasters followed, in the course of which two men were carried off by Indians and never again seen, and others fled for home. Those remaining, having still much ammunition and the horses, continued their hunt, chiefly upon the Green and Cumberland Rivers, and in due time brought together another store of peltries, almost as extensive as that despoiled by the savages.

Not long after the robbery, when the Long Hunters were upon Green River, one of the parties into which the band was divided were going into camp for the night, when a singular noise was heard proceeding from a considerable distance in the forest. The leader, Caspar Mausker, commanded silence on the part of his comrades, and himself crept cautiously from tree to tree in the direction of the sound. Imagine his surprise and amusement to find "a man bare-headed, stretched flat upon his back on a deerskin spread on the ground, singing merrily at the top of his voice!" The singer was our hero, Daniel Boone, who, regardless of possible Indian neighbors, was thus enjoying himself while awaiting Squire's belated return to camp. Like most woodsmen of his day and ours, Boone was fond of singing, in his rude way, as well as of relating tales of stirring adventure. In such manner were many hours whiled away around the camp-fires of wilderness hunters.

The Boones at once joined and spent some time with the Long Hunters, no doubt delighted at this opportunity of once more mingling with men of their kind. Among their amusements was that of naming rivers, creeks, and hills after members of the party; many of these names are still preserved upon the map of Kentucky. At one time they discovered that some French hunters from the Illinois country had recently visited a lick to kill buffaloes for their tongues and tallow, which they had loaded into a keel-boat and taken down the Cumberland. In after years one of the Long Hunters declared that this wholesale slaughter was so great "that one could walk for several hundred yards in and around the lick on buffaloes' skulls and bones, with which the whole flat around the lick was bleached."

It was not until August that the Long Hunters returned to their homes, after a profitable absence of eleven months. But the Boone brothers left their comrades in March and headed for the Yadkin, with horses now well laden with spoils of the chase. They were deeply in debt for their latest supplies, but were returning in light heart, cheered with the prospect of settling their accounts and being able to revisit Kentucky in good condition. But in Powell's Valley, near Cumberland Gap, where they might well have supposed that small chance of danger remained, they were suddenly set upon by a war party of Northern Indians who had been raiding the white settlers as well as their Southern foes, the Cherokees and Catawbas. Roughly handled and robbed of their packs, the unfortunate hunters reached the Yadkin in no happy frame of mind. Daniel had been absent for two years, and was now poorer than when he left home. He used to say, however, in after years, that having at last seen Kentucky, his ideal of an earthly paradise, that served as solace for his woes.

CHAPTER VIII

THE HERO OF CLINCH VALLEY

WHILE Daniel Boone had been hunting and exploring amid the deep forests and waving greenswards of Kentucky, important events had been taking place in the settlements. The colonists along the Atlantic tidewater had become so crowded that there were no longer any free lands in that region; and settlers' cabins in the western uplands of Pennsylvania, Maryland, the Carolinas, and Georgia had so multiplied that now much of the best land there had also been taken up. The far-outlying frontier upon which the Boones and Bryans had reared their rude log huts nearly a quarter of a century before, no longer abounded in game and in free pastures for roving herds; indeed, the frontier was now pushed forward to the west-flowing streams—to the head waters of the Watauga, Clinch, Powell, French Broad, Holston, and Nolichucky, all of them affluents of the Tennessee, and to the Monongahela and other tributaries of the upper Ohio.

The rising tide of population demanded more room to the westward. The forbidding mountain-ranges had long hemmed in the restless borderers; but the dark-skinned wilderness tribes had formed a still more serious barrier, as, with rifles and tomahawks purchased from white traders, they terrorized the slowly advancing outposts of civilization. With the French government no longer in control of Canada and the region east of the Mississippi—although French-Canadian woodsmen were freely employed by the British Indian Department—with the consequent quieting of Indian forays, with increased knowledge of the over-mountain passes, and with the strong push of population from behind, there had arisen a general desire to scale the hills, and beyond them to seek exemption from tax-gatherers, free lands, and the abundant game concerning which the Kentucky hunters had brought glowing reports.

Upon the defeat of the French, the English king had issued a proclamation (1763) forbidding his "loving subjects" to settle to the west of the mountains. The home government was no doubt actuated in this by two motives: first, a desire to preserve the wilderness for the benefit of the growing fur trade, which brought wealth to many London merchants; second, a fear that borderers who pushed beyond the mountains might not only be beyond the reach of English trade, but also beyond English political control. But the frontiersmen were already too far distant to have much regard for royal proclamations. The king's command appears to have had no more effect than had he, like one of his predecessors, bade the ocean tide rise no higher.

In 1768, at Fort Stanwix, N. Y., the Iroquois of that province, whose war parties had raided much of the country between the Hudson and the Mississippi, surrendered what shadowy rights they might be supposed to have over all lands lying between the Ohio and the Tennessee. Meanwhile, at the South, the Cherokees had agreed to a frontier which opened to settlement eastern Kentucky and Tennessee.

But, without waiting for these treaties, numerous schemes had been proposed in England and the Atlantic coast colonies for the settlement of Kentucky and the lands of the upper Ohio. Most of these projects failed, even the more promising of them being checked by the opening of the Revolutionary War; but their existence showed how general was the desire of English colonists to occupy those fertile Western lands which explorers like Gist, Washington, the Boones, and the Long Hunters had now made familiar to the world. The new treaties strengthened this desire, so that when Daniel and Squire Boone reached their homes upon the Yadkin the subject of Western settlement was uppermost in the minds of the people.

The land excitement was, however, less intense in North Carolina than in the Valley of Virginia and other mountain troughs to the north and northeast. At Boone's home there was unrest of a more serious character. The tax-gatherers were arousing great popular discontent because of unlawful and extortionate demands, and in some cases Governor Tryon had come to blows with the regulators who stood for the people's rights.

For two and a half years after his return Boone quietly conducted his little farm, and, as of old, made long hunting trips in autumn and winter, occasionally venturing—sometimes alone, sometimes with one or two companions—far west into Kentucky, once visiting French Lick, on the Cumberland, where he found several French hunters. There is reason to believe that in 1772 he moved to the Watauga Valley, but after living there for a time went back to the Yadkin. Early in the following year he accompanied Benjamin Cutbirth and others as far as the present Jessamine County, Ky., and from this trip returned fired with quickened zeal for making a settlement in the new country.

The spring and summer were spent in active preparations. He enlisted the cooperation of Captain William Russell, the principal pioneer in the Clinch Valley; several of the Bryans, whose settlement was now sixty-five miles distant, also agreed to join him; and five other families in his own neighborhood engaged to join the expedition.

The Bryan party, numbering forty men, some of them from the Valley of Virginia and Powell's Valley, were not to be accompanied by their families, as they preferred to go in advance and prepare homes before making a final move. But Boone and the other men of the upper Yadkin took with them their wives and children; most of them sold their farms, as did Boone, thus burning their bridges behind them. Arranging to meet the Bryan contingent in Powell's Valley, Boone's party left for the West upon the twenty-fifth of September, 1773—fifty-six years after old George Boone had departed from England for the Pennsylvania frontier near Philadelphia, and twenty-three after the family had set out for the new southwest frontier on the Yadkin.

Reaching Powell's, Boone went into camp to await the rear party, his riding and pack-horses hoppled and belled, after the custom of such caravans, and their small herd of cattle properly guarded in a meadow. His eldest son, James, now a boy of sixteen years, was sent with two men, with pack-animals, across country to notify Russell and to secure some flour and farming tools. They were returning laden, in company with Russell's son Henry, a year older than James, two of Russell's negro slaves, and two or three white workpeople, when, missing their path, they went into camp for the night only three miles from Boone's quarters. At daybreak they were attacked by a Shawnese war party and all killed except a white laborer and a negro. This pathetic tragedy created such consternation among the movers that, despite Boone's entreaties to go forward, all of them returned to Virginia and Carolina. Daniel and his family, no longer having a home on the Yadkin, would not retreat, and took up their quarters in an empty cabin upon the farm of Captain David Gass, seven or eight miles from Russell's, upon Clinch River. Throughout this sorrowful winter the Boones were supported from their stock of cattle and by means of Daniel's unerring rifle.

It was long before the intrepid pioneers could again take up their line of march. Ever since the Bouquet treaty of 1764 there had been more or less disturbance upon the frontiers. During all these years, although there was no open warfare between whites and reds, many scores of lives had been lost. Indians had wantonly plundered and murdered white men, and the latter had been quite as merciless toward the savages. Whenever a member of one race met a man of the other the rifle was apt to be at once brought into play. Meanwhile, armed parties of surveyors and land speculators were swarming into Kentucky, notching the trees for landmarks, and giving evidence to apprehensive tribesmen that the hordes of civilization were upon them. In 1773 George Rogers Clark, afterward the most famous of border leaders, had staked a claim at the mouth of Fishing Creek, on the Ohio; Washington had, this summer, descended the river to the same point; while at the Falls of the Ohio, and upon interior waters of the Kentucky wilderness, other parties were laying ambitious plans for the capitals of new colonies.

In the following spring the Cherokees and Shawnese, now wrought to a high pitch of ill temper, combined for onslaughts on the advancing frontiersmen. The wanton murder by border ruffians of Chief John Logan's family, near Mingo Junction, on the Ohio, was the match which, in early summer, fired the tinder. The Mingos, ablaze with the fire of vengeance, carried the war-pipe through the neighboring villages; runners were sent in every direction to rouse the tribes; tomahawks were unearthed, war-posts were planted; messages of defiance were sent to the "Virginians," as all frontiersmen were generally called by the Western Indians; and in a few days the border war to which history has given the name of Lord Dunmore, then governor of Virginia, was in full swing from Cumberland Gap to Fort Pitt, from the Alleghanies to the Wabash.

Its isolation at first protected the Valley of the Clinch. The commandant of the southwest militia—which comprised every boy or man capable of bearing arms—was Colonel William Preston; under him was Major Arthur Campbell; the principal man in the Clinch Valley was Boone's friend, Russell. When, in June, the border captains were notified by Lord Dunmore that the war was now on, forts were erected in each of the mountain valleys, and scouts sent out along the trails and streams to ascertain the whereabouts of the enemy.

There were in Kentucky, at this time, several surveying parties which could not obtain news by way of the Ohio because of the blockade maintained by the Shawnese. It became necessary to notify them overland, and advise their retreat to the settlements by way of Cumberland Gap. Russell having been ordered by Preston to employ "two faithful woodsmen" for this purpose, chose Daniel Boone and Michael Stoner. "If they are alive," wrote Russell to his colonel, "it is indisputable but Boone must find them." Leaving the Clinch on June twenty-seventh, the two envoys were at Harrodsburg before July eighth. There they found James Harrod and thirty-four other men laying off a large town,* in which they proposed to give

* Previous to this there had been built in Kentucky many hunters' camps, also a few isolated cabins by "improvers"; but Harrodsburg (at first called "Harrodstown") was the first permanent settlement, thus having nearly a year's start of Boonesborough. June 16, 1774, is the date given by Collins and other chroniclers for the actual settlement by Harrod.

each inhabitant a half-acre in-lot and a ten-acre out-lot. Boone, who had small capacity for business, but in land was something of a speculator, registered as a settler, and in company with a neighbor put up a cabin for his future occupancy. This done, he and Stoner hurried on down the Kentucky River to its mouth, and thence to the Falls of the Ohio (site of Louisville), notifying several bands of surveyors and town-builders of their danger. After an absence of sixty-one days they were back again upon the Clinch, having traveled eight hundred miles through a practically unbroken forest, experienced many dangers from Indians, and overcome natural difficulties almost without number.

Meanwhile Lord Dunmore, personally unpopular but an energetic and competent military manager, had sent out an army of nearly three thousand backwoodsmen against the Shawnese north of the Ohio. One wing of this army, led by the governor himself, went by way of Fort Pitt and descended the Ohio; among its members was George Rogers Clark. The other wing, commanded by General Andrew Lewis, included the men of the Southwest, eleven hundred strong; they were to descend the Great Kanawha and rendezvous with the northern wing at Point Pleasant, at the junction of the Kanawha and the Ohio.

When Boone arrived upon the Clinch he found that Russell and most of the other militiamen of the district had departed upon the campaign. With a party of recruits, the great hunter started out to overtake the expedition, but was met by orders to return and aid in defending his own valley; for the drawing off of the militia by Dunmore had left the southwest frontiers in weak condition. During September the settlers upon the Clinch suffered much apprehension; the depredations of the tribesmen were not numerous, but several men were either wounded or captured.

In a letter written upon the sixth of October, Major Campbell gives a list of forts upon the Clinch: "Blackmore's, sixteen men, Sergeant Moore commanding; Moore's, twenty miles above, twenty men, Lieutenant Boone commanding; Russell's, four miles above, twenty men, Sergeant W. Poage commanding; Glade Hollow, twelve miles above, fifteen men, Sergeant John Dunkin commanding; Elk Garden, fourteen miles above, eighteen men, Sergeant John Kinkead commanding; Maiden Spring, twenty-three miles above, five men, Sergeant John Crane commanding; Whitton's Big Crab Orchard, twelve miles above, three men, Ensign John Campbell, of Rich Valley, commanding." During this month Boone and his little garrison made frequent sallies against the enemy, and now and then fought brief but desperate skirmishes. He appears to have been by far the most active commander in the valley, and when neighboring forts were attacked his party of well-trained riflemen generally furnished the relief necessary to raise the siege. "Mr. Boone," writes Campbell to Preston, "is very diligent at Castle's-woods, and keeps up good order." His conduct is frequently alluded to in the military correspondence of that summer; Campbell and other leaders exhibited in their references to our hero a respectful and even deferential tone. An eye-witness of some of these stirring scenes has left us a description of Daniel

Boone, now forty years of age, in which it is stated that his was then a familiar figure throughout the valley as he hurried to and fro upon his military duties "dressed in deerskin colored black, and his hair plaited and clubbed up."

Upon the tenth of October, Cornstalk, a famous Shawnese chief, taking advantage of Dunmore's failure to join the southern wing, led against Lewis's little army encamped at Point Pleasant a thousand picked warriors gathered from all parts of the Northwest. Here, upon the wooded eminence at the junction of the two rivers, was waged from dawn until dusk one of the most bloody and stubborn hand-to-hand battles ever fought between Indians and whites. It is hard to say who displayed the best generalship, Cornstalk or Lewis. The American savage was a splendid fighter; although weak in discipline he could competently plan a battle. The tactics of surprise were his chief resource, and these are legitimate even in civilized warfare; but he could also make a determined contest in the open, and when, as at Point Pleasant, the opposing numbers were nearly equal, the result was often slow of determination. Desperately courageous, pertinacious, with a natural aptitude for war combined with consummate treachery, cruelty, and cunning, it is small wonder that the Indian long offered a formidable barrier to the advance of civilization. In early Virginia, John Smith noticed that in Indian warfare the whites won at the expense of losses far beyond those suffered by the tribesmen; and here at Point Pleasant, while the "Long Knives" * gained the day, the number of their dead and wounded was double that of the casualties sustained by Cornstalk's painted band.

---

* The Indians had called the Americans "Knifemen," "Long Knives," or "Big Knives," from the earliest historic times; but it was not until about the middle of the eighteenth century that the Virginia colonists began to make record of the use of this epithet by the Indians with whom they came in contact. It was then commonly supposed that it grew out of the use of swords by the frontier militiamen, and this is the meaning still given in dictionaries; but it has been made apparent by Albert Matthews, writing in the New York Nation, March 14, 1901, that the epithet originated in the fact that Englishmen used knives as distinguished from the early stone tools of the Indians. The French introduced knives into America previous to the English, but apparently the term was used only by Indians within the English sphere of influence.

The victory at Point Pleasant practically closed the war upon the border. Boone had been made a captain in response to a popular petition that the hero of Clinch Valley be thus honored, and was given charge of the three lower forts; but there followed only a few alarms, and upon the twentieth of November he and his brother militiamen of the region received their discharge. The war had cost Virginia £10,000 sterling, many valuable lives had been sacrificed, and an incalculable amount of suffering and privation had been occasioned all along the three hundred and fifty miles of American frontier. But the Shawnese had been humbled, the Cherokees had retired behind the new border line, and a lasting peace appeared to be assured.

In the following January Captain Boone, true son of the wilderness, was celebrating his freedom from duties incident to war's alarms by a solitary hunt upon the banks of Kentucky River.

CHAPTER IX

THE SETTLEMENT OF KENTUCKY

KENTUCKY had so long been spasmodically occupied and battled over by Shawnese, Iroquois, and Cherokees, that it can not be said that any of them had well-defined rights over its soil. Not until white men appeared anxious to settle there did the tribes begin to assert their respective claims, in the hope of gaining presents at the treaties whereat they were asked to make cessions. The whites, on their part, when negotiating for purchases, were well aware of the shadowy character of these claims; but, when armed with a signed deed of cession, they had something tangible upon which thenceforth to base their own claims of proprietorship. There was therefore much insincerity upon both sides. It is well to understand this situation in studying the history of Kentucky settlement.

Colonel Richard Henderson was one of the

principal judges in North Carolina, a scholarly, talented man, eminent in the legal profession; although but thirty-nine years of age, he wielded much influence. Knowing and respecting Daniel Boone, Henderson was much impressed by the former's enthusiastic reports concerning the soil, climate, and scenery of Kentucky; and, acting solely upon this information, resolved to establish a colony in that attractive country. He associated with himself three brothers, Nathaniel, David, and Thomas Hart, the last-named of whom in later life wrote that he "had known Boone of old, when poverty and distress held him fast by the hand; and in those wretched circumstances he had ever found him a noble and generous soul, despising everything mean." Their proposed colony was styled Transylvania, and the association of proprietors the Transylvania Company.

It will be remembered that in the treaty of Fort Stanwix (1768) the Iroquois of New York had ceded to the English crown their pretensions to lands lying between the Ohio and the Tennessee. The Transylvania Company, however, applied to the Cherokees, because this was the tribe commanding the path from Virginia and the Carolinas to Kentucky. In March, 1775, a great council was held at Sycamore Shoals, on the Watauga River, between the company and twelve hundred Cherokees who had been brought in for the purpose by Boone. For $50,000 worth of cloths, clothing, utensils, ornaments, and firearms, the Indians ceded to Henderson and his partners an immense grant including all the country lying between the Kentucky and Cumberland Rivers, also a path of approach from the east, through Powell's Valley. At this council were some of the most prominent Cherokee chiefs and southwestern frontiersmen.

When the goods came to be distributed among the Indians it was found that, although they filled a large cabin and looked very tempting in bulk, there was but little for each warrior, and great dissatisfaction arose. One Cherokee, whose portion was a shirt, declared that in one day, upon this land, he could have killed deer enough to buy such a garment; to surrender his hunting-ground for this trifle naturally seemed to him a bad bargain. For the safety of the pioneers the chiefs could give no guarantee; they warned Boone, who appears to have acted as spokesman for the company, that "a black cloud hung over this land," war-paths crossed it from north to south, and settlers would surely get killed; for such results the Cherokees must not be held responsible.

This was not promising. Neither was the news, now received, that Governors Martin of North Carolina, and Dunmore of Virginia had both of them issued proclamations against the great purchase. The former had called Henderson and his partners an "infamous Company of Land Pyrates"; and they were notified that this movement was in violation of the king's proclamation of 1763, forbidding Western settlements.

The company, relying upon popular sympathy and their great distance from tide-water seats of government, proceeded without regard to these proclamations. Boone, at the head of a party of about thirty enlisted men, some of them the best backwoodsmen in the country,* was sent ahead to mark a path through the forest to Kentucky River, and there establish a capital for the new colony. They encountered many difficulties, especially when traveling through cane-brakes and brush; and once, while asleep, were attacked by Indians, who killed a negro servant and wounded two of the party. Boone won hearty commendation for his skill and courage throughout the expedition, which finally arrived at its destination on the sixth of April. This was Big Lick, on Kentucky River, just below the mouth of Otter Creek. Here it was decided to build a town

* The names of this party of Kentucky pioneers, as preserved by tradition, are worth presenting in our record, for many of them afterward became prominent in the annals of the West: Squire Boone, Edward Bradley, James Bridges, William Bush, Samuel Coburn, Colonel Richard Calloway, Captain Crabtree, Benjamin Cutbirth, David Gass, John Hart, William Hays (son-in-law of Daniel Boone), William Hicks, Edmund Jennings, Thomas Johnson, John Kennedy, John King, William Miller, William Moore, James Nall, James Peeke, Bartlet Searcy, Reuben Searcy, Michael Stoner, Samuel Tate, Oswell Towns, Captain William Twitty (wounded at Rockcastle), John Vardeman, and Felix Walker (also wounded at Rockcastle). Mrs. Hays, Boone's daughter, traveled with her husband; a negro woman accompanied Calloway, and a negro man (killed at Rockcastle) was with Twitty.

to be called Boonesborough, to serve as the capital of Transylvania. The site was "a plain on the south side of the river, wherein was a lick with sulphur springs strongly impregnated."

To Felix Walker, one of the pioneers, we are indebted for the details of this notable colonizing expedition, set forth in a narrative which is still preserved. "On entering the plain," he writes, "we were permitted to view a very interesting and romantic sight. A number of buffaloes, of all sizes, supposed to be between two and three hundred, made off from the lick in every direction: some running, some walking, others loping slowly and carelessly, with young calves playing, skipping, and bounding through the plain. Such a sight some of us never saw before, nor perhaps ever may again." A fort was commenced, and a few cabins "strung along the river-bank;" but it was long before the stronghold was completed, for, now that the journey was at an end, Boone's men had become callous to danger.

Meanwhile Henderson was proceeding slowly from the settlements with thirty men and several wagons loaded with goods and tools. Delayed from many causes, they at last felt obliged to leave the encumbering wagons in Powell's Valley. Pushing forward, they were almost daily met by parties of men and boys returning home from Kentucky bearing vague reports of Indian forays. This resulted in Henderson losing many of his own followers from desertion. Arriving at Boonesborough on the twentieth of April, the relief party was "saluted by a running fire of about twenty-five guns." Some of Boone's men had, in the general uneasiness, also deserted, and others had scattered throughout the woods, hunting, exploring, or surveying on their own account.

The method of surveying then in vogue upon the Western frontier was of the crudest, although it must be acknowledged that any system more formal might, at that stage of our country's growth, have prevented rapid settlement. Each settler or land speculator was practically his own surveyor. With a compass and a chain, a few hours' work would suffice to mark the boundaries of a thousand-acre tract. There were as yet no adequate maps of the country, and claims overlapped each other in the most bewildering manner. A speculator who "ran out" a hundred thousand acres might, without knowing it, include in his domain a half-dozen claims previously surveyed by modest settlers who wanted but a hundred acres each. A man who paid the land-office fees might "patent" any land he pleased and have it recorded, the colony, and later the State, only guaranteeing such entries as covered land not already patented. This overlapping, conscious or unconscious, at last became so perplexing that thousands of vexatious lawsuits followed, some of which are still unsettled; and even to-day in Kentucky there are lands whose ownership is actually unknown, which pay no taxes and support only squatters who can not be turned out—possibly some of it, lying between patented tracts, by chance has never been entered at all. Nobody can now say. Thus it was that we find our friend Daniel Boone quickly transformed from a wilderness hunter into a frontier surveyor. Before Henderson's arrival he had laid off the town site

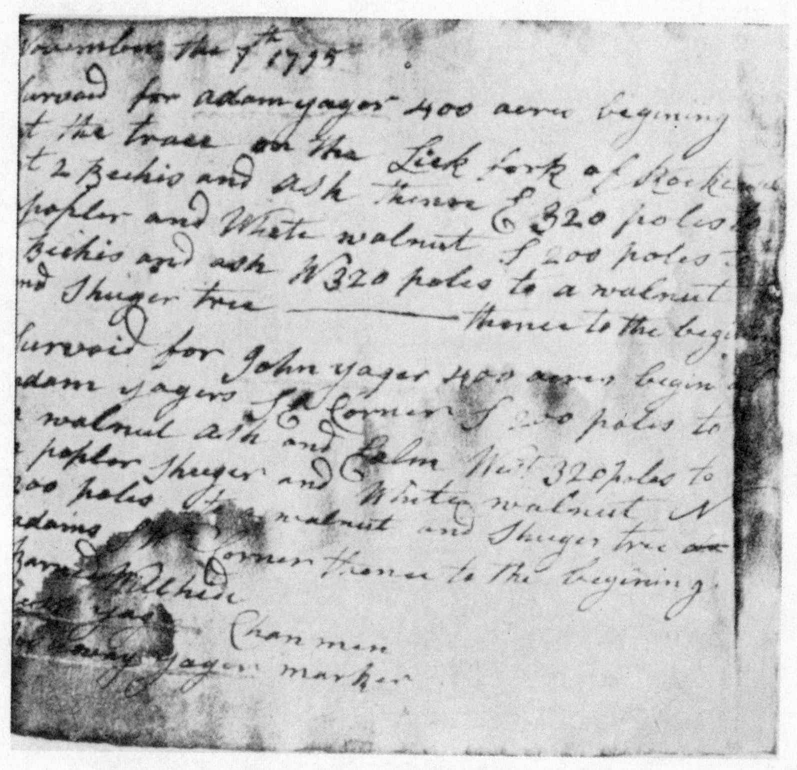

the 7th 1775

urvaid for adam yager 400 acres begining
t the trace on the Lick fork of Rocke
t 2 Beckis and ash thence E 320 poles
poplar and White walnut S 200 poles
Beckis and ash W 320 poles to a walnut
nd Shuger tree ——— thence to the begi
urvaid for John yager 400 acres begin
dam yagers SE Corner S 200 poles to
walnut ash and Elm West 320 poles to
poplar Shuger and White walnut N
200 poles to a walnut and Shuger tree
adams Corner thence to the begining.

Chan men

yager marker

A SURVEY NOTE BY BOONE.

Reduced facsimile from his field-books in possession of Wisconsin State Historical Society.

into lots of two acres each. These were now drawn at a public lottery; while those who wished larger tracts within the neighborhood were able to obtain them by promising to plant a crop of corn and pay to the Transylvania Company a quit-rent of two English shillings for each hundred acres.

There were now four settlements in the Transylvania grant: Boonesborough; Harrodsburg, fifty miles west, with about a hundred men; Boiling Spring, some six or seven miles from Harrodsburg; and St. Asaph. The crown lands to the north and east of the Kentucky, obtained by the Fort Stanwix treaty, contained two small settlements; forty miles north of Boonesborough was Hinkson's, later known as Ruddell's Station, where were about nineteen persons; lower down the Kentucky, also on the north side, was Willis Lee's settlement, near the present Frankfort; and ranging at will through the crown lands were several small parties of "land-jobbers," surveyors, and explorers, laying off the claims of militia officers who had fought in the Indian wars, and here and there building cabins to indicate possession.

Henderson had no sooner arrived than he prepared for a convention, at which the people should adopt a form of government for the colony and elect officers. This was held at Boonesborough, in the open air, under a gigantic elm, during the week commencing Tuesday, the twenty-third of May. There were eighteen delegates, representing each of the four settlements south of the Kentucky. Among them were Daniel and Squire Boone, the former of whom proposed laws for the preservation of game and for improving the breed of horses; to the latter fell the presentation of rules for preserving the cattle-ranges. The compact finally agreed upon between the colonists and the proprietors declared " the powers of the one and the liberties of the others," and was " the earliest form of government in the region west of the Alleghanies." It provided for " perfect religious freedom and general toleration," militia and judicial systems, and complete liberty on the part of the settlers to conduct colonial affairs according to their needs. This liberal and well-digested plan appeared to please both Henderson and the settlers.

But the opposition of the governors, the objections raised by the Assembly of Virginia, of which Kentucky was then a part,* and finally, the outbreak of the Revolution, which put an end to proprietary governments in America, caused the downfall of the Transylvania Company. The Boonesborough legislative convention met but once more—in December, to elect a surveyor-general.

The May meeting had no sooner adjourned than Transylvania began again to lose its population. Few of the pioneers who had come out with Boone and Henderson, or had since wandered into the district, were genuine home-seekers. Many appear to have been mere adventurers, out for the excitement of the expedition and to satisfy their curiosity, who either returned home or wandered farther into the woods to seek fresh experiences of wild life; others had deliberately intended first to stake out claims in the neighborhood of the new settlements and then return home to look after their

* It was then within the far-stretching boundaries of Fincastle County. Kentucky was set apart as a county, December 31, 1776.

crops, and perhaps move to Kentucky in the autumn; others there were who, far removed from their families, proved restless; while many became uneasy because of Indian outrages, reports of which soon began to be circulated. Henderson wrote cheerful letters to his partners at home, describing the country as a paradise; but by the end of June, when Boone returned to the East for salt, Harrodsburg and Boiling Spring were almost deserted, while Boonesborough could muster but ten or twelve "guns," as men or boys capable of fighting Indians were called in the militia rolls.

The infant colony of Kentucky had certainly reached a crisis in its career. Game was rapidly becoming more scarce, largely because of careless, inexperienced hunters who wounded more than they killed, and killed more than was needed for food; the frightened buffaloes had now receded so far west that they were several days' journey from Boonesborough. Yet game was still the staff of life. Captain Floyd, the surveyor-general, wrote to Colonel Preston: "I must hunt or starve."

The Settlement of Kentucky

As the summer wore away and crops in the Eastern settlements were gathered, there was a considerable increase in the population. Many men who, in later days, were to exert a powerful influence in Kentucky now arrived—George Rogers Clark, the principal Western hero of the Revolution; Simon Kenton, famous throughout the border as hunter, scout, and Indian fighter; Benjamin Logan, William Whitley, the Lewises, Campbells, Christians, Prestons, MacDowells, McAfees, Hite, Bowman, Randolph, Todd, McClellan, Benton, Patterson—all of them names familiar in Western history.

In the first week of September Boone arrived with his wife and family and twenty young men—"twenty-one guns," the report reads; Squire and his family soon followed; four Bryans, their brothers-in-law, came at the head of thirty men from the Yadkin; and, at the same time, Harrodsburg was reached by several other families who had, like the Boones, come on horseback through Cumberland Gap and Powell's Valley. This powerful reenforcement of pioneers, most of whom proposed to stay, had largely been attracted by Henderson's advertisements in Virginia newspapers offering terms of settlement on Transylvania lands. "Any person," said the announcement, "who will settle on and inhabit the same before the first day of June, 1776, shall have the privilege of taking up and surveying for himself five hundred acres, and for each tithable person he may carry with him and settle there, two hundred and fifty acres, on the payment of fifty shillings sterling per hundred, subject to a yearly quit-rent of two shillings, like money, to commence in the year 1780." Toward the end of November Henderson himself, who had gone on a visit to Carolina, returned with forty men, one of whom was Colonel Arthur Campbell, a prominent settler in the Holston Valley.

This increase of population, which had been noticeable throughout the autumn and early winter, received a sudden check, however, two days before Christmas, when the Indians, who had been friendly for several months past, began again to annoy settlers, several being either killed or carried into captivity. This gave rise to a fresh panic, in the course of which many fled to the east of the mountains.

During the year about five hundred persons from the frontiers of Pennsylvania, Virginia, and North Carolina had visited and explored Kentucky; but now, at the close of December, the population of all the settlements did not aggregate over two hundred. The recent outbreak had much to do with this situation of affairs; but there were other causes conspiring to disturb the minds of the people and postpone the growth of settlement—the clashing of interests between the Transylvania Company and the governors of Virginia and North Carolina, uncertainty as to the possibilities of a general Indian war, the threatened rupture between the colonies and the English crown, and the alarming scarcity of provisions and ammunition throughout Kentucky.

Nevertheless, over nine hundred entries had been made in the Transylvania land-office at Boonesborough, embracing 560,000 acres, and most of these tracts were waiting to be surveyed; two hundred and thirty acres of corn had been successfully raised; horses, hogs, and poultry had been introduced, and apple- and peach-trees had been started at several settlements. The germ of a colony was firmly planted, laws had been made, the militia had been organized, civil and military officers had been commissioned, and in the face of several slight Indian attacks the savages had been repelled and the country maintained. Most promising of all, there were now twelve women in the country, all of them heads of families.

The principal pioneers were nearly all of sturdy Scotch-Irish blood, men of sterling merit, intensely devoted to the cause of American liberty, and destined to contribute powerfully to its aid in the great war which had now begun, and concerning which messengers from over the mountains had during the year brought them scanty information.

CHAPTER X

TWO YEARS OF DARKNESS

WITH the opening of the year 1776 Daniel and Squire Boone were employed for several weeks as hunters or assistants to a party of surveyors sent by the Transylvania Company to the Falls of the Ohio, in the vicinity of which Henderson and his friends had taken up seventy thousand acres of land. They met no Indians and saw plenty of game; but returned to find that the settlers were indignant because of this wholesale preemption by the proprietors of the colony in a neighborhood where it was now felt the chief city in Kentucky was sure to be planted. In response to this clamor Henderson promised that hereafter, in that locality, only small tracts should be granted to individuals, and that a town should at once be laid out at the Falls; but the scanty supply of powder and provisions, and the company's growing troubles with the Virginia Assembly, prevented the execution of this project.

In the spring newcomers everywhere appeared. In order to please the people of Harrodsburg, now the largest settlement, who were disposed to be critical, the company's land-office was moved thither, and it at once entered upon a flourishing business. Not only did many Virginians and Carolinians come in on horseback over the "Wilderness Road," as the route through Cumberland Gap was now styled, but hundreds also descended the Ohio in boats from the new settlements on the Monongahela, and from those farther east in Pennsylvania.

While the horsemen of the Wilderness Road generally settled in Transylvania, those journeying by boat were chiefly interested in the crown lands north of the Kentucky; through these they ranged at will, building rude pens, half-faced cabins, and log huts, as convenience dictated, and planting small crops of corn in order to preempt their claims. The majority, however, after making sometimes as many as twenty such claims each, often upon land already surveyed on militia officers' warrants, returned home at the close of the season, seeking to sell their fictitious holdings to actual settlers. Of course the unscrupulous conduct of these "claim-jumping" speculators led to numerous quarrels. John Todd, of Harrodsburg, wrote to a friend: "I am afraid to lose sight of my house lest some invader should take possession."

It was difficult, even for those who came to settle, to get down to hard work during those earliest years. Never was there a more beautiful region than the Kentucky wilderness. Both old and new settlers were fond of roaming through this wonderland of forests and glades and winding rivers, where the nights were cool and refreshing and the days filled with harmonies of sound and sight and smell. Hill and valley, timberland and thicket, meadow and prairie, grasslands and cane-brake—these abounded on every hand, in happy distribution of light and shadow. The soil was extremely fertile; there were many open spots fitted for immediate cultivation; the cattle-ranges were of the best, for nowhere was cane more abundant; game was more plentiful than men's hopes had ever before conceived—of turkeys, bears, deer, and buffaloes it seemed, for a time, as if the supply must always far excelled any possible demand. It is small wonder that the imaginations of the pioneers were fired with dreams of the future, that they saw in fancy great cities springing up in this new world of the West, and wealth pouring into the laps of those who could first obtain a foothold. Thus, in that beautiful spring of 1776, did Kentuckians revel in the pleasures of hope, and cast to the winds all thought of the peril and toil by which alone can man conquer a savage-haunted wilderness.

But the "dark cloud" foretold at the Watauga treaty soon settled upon the land. Incited by British agents—for the Revolution was now on—the Cherokees on the south and the Shawnese and Mingos on the north declared war upon the American borderers. The Kentuckians were promptly warned by messengers from the East. The "cabiners," as claim speculators were called by actual settlers; the wandering fur-traders, most of whom were shabby rascals, whose example corrupted the savages, and whose conduct often led to outbreaks of race hostility; and the irresponsible hunters, who were recklessly killing or frightening off the herds of game—all of these classes began, with the mutterings of conflict, to draw closer to the settlements; while many hurried back to their old homes, carrying exaggerated reports of the situation.

Meanwhile, opposition to the Transylvania proprietors was fast developing. The settlers in the Harrodsburg neighborhood held a convention in June and sent Colonel George Rogers Clark and Captain John Gabriel Jones as delegates to the Virginia Convention with a petition to that body to make Kentucky a county of Virginia. This project was bitterly opposed by Henderson; but upon the adoption by Congress, in July, of the Declaration of Independence, there was small chance left for the recognition of any proprietary government. When the new Virginia legislature met in the autumn, the petition of the "inhabitants of Kentuckie" was granted, and a county government organized.* David Robinson was appointed county lieutenant, John Bowman colonel, Anthony Bledsoe and George Rogers Clark majors, and Daniel Boone, James Harrod, John Todd, and Benjamin Logan captains.

It was not until July that the Kentuckians fully realized the existence of an Indian war. During that month several hunters, surveyors, and travelers were killed in various parts of the district. The situation promised so badly that Colonel William Russell, of the Holston Valley, commandant of the southwestern Virginia militia, advised the immediate abandonment of Kentucky. Such advice fell upon unheeding ears in the case of men like Boone and his companions, although many of the less valorous were quick to retire beyond the mountains.

On Sunday, the seventeenth of July, an incident occurred at Boonesborough which created wide-spread consternation. Jemima, the second daughter of Daniel Boone, aged fourteen years, together with two girl

* It was, however, not until November, 1778, that the legislature formally declared the Transylvania Company's claims null and void.

friends, Betsey and Fanny Calloway, sixteen and fourteen respectively, were paddling in a canoe upon the Kentucky. Losing control of their craft in the swift current, not over a quarter of a mile from the settlement, they were swept near the north bank, when five Shawnese braves, hiding in the bushes, waded out and captured them. The screams of the girls alarmed the settlers, who sallied forth in hot pursuit of the kidnappers.

The mounted men, under Colonel Calloway, father of two of the captives, pushed forward to Lower Blue Licks, hoping to cut off the Indians as they crossed the Licking River on their way to the Shawnese towns in Ohio, whither it was correctly supposed they were fleeing. Boone headed the footmen, who followed closely on the trail of the fugitives, which had been carefully marked by the girls, who, with the self-possession of true borderers, furtively scattered broken twigs and scraps of clothing as they were hurried along through the forest by their grim captors. After a two days' chase, Boone's party caught up with the unsuspecting savages some thirty-five miles from

Boonesborough, and by dint of a skilful dash recaptured the young women, unharmed. Two of the Shawnese were killed and the others fled into the woods. Calloway's horsemen met no foe.

Although few other attacks were reported during the summer or autumn, the people were in a continual state of apprehension, neglected their crops, and either huddled in the neighborhood of the settlements, or "stations" as they were called, or abandoned the country altogether. In the midst of this uneasiness Floyd wrote to his friend Preston, in Virginia, urging that help be sent to the distressed colony: "They all seem deaf to anything we can say to dissuade them. . . . I think more than three hundred men have left the country since I came out, and not one has arrived, except a few *cabiners* down the Ohio. I want to return as much as any man can do; but if I leave the country now there is scarcely one single man who will not follow the example. When I think of the deplorable condition a few helpless families are likely to be in, I conclude to sell my life as dearly as I can in

FORT BOONESBOROUGH.

Drawn from Henderson's plans and other historical data by George W. Ranck; reduced from the latter's "Boonesborough" (Filson Club Publications, No. 16).

their defense rather than make an ignominious escape."

Seven stations had now been abandoned —Huston's, on the present site of Paris; Hinkson's, on the Licking; Bryan's, on the Elkhorn; Lee's, on the Kentucky; Harrod's, or the Boiling Spring settlement; Whitley's, and Logan's. But three remained occupied —McClellan's, Harrodsburg, and Boonesborough. Up to this time none of the Kentucky stations had been fortified; there had been some unfinished work at Boonesborough, but it was soon allowed to fall into decay. Work was now resumed at all three of the occupied settlements; this consisted simply of connecting the cabins, which faced an open square, by lines of palisades. It was only at McClellan's, however, that even this slender protection was promptly completed; at Boonesborough and Harrodsburg the work, although but a task of a few days, dragged slowly, and was not finished for several months. It was next to impossible for Boone and the other militia captains to induce men to labor at the common defenses in time of peace.

Great popular interest was taken by the people of the Carolinas, Virginia, and Pennsylvania in the fate of the Kentucky settlements, whither so many prominent borderers from those States had moved. The frantic appeals for help sent out by Floyd, Logan, and McGary, and expressed in person by George Rogers Clark, awakened keen sympathy; but the demands of Washington's army were now so great, in battles for national liberty upon the Atlantic coast, that little could be spared for the Western settlers. During the summer a small supply of powder was sent out by Virginia to Captain Boone; in the autumn Harrod and Logan rode to the Holston and obtained from the military authorities a packhorse-load of lead; and in the closing days of the year Clark arrived at Limestone (now Maysville), on the Ohio, with a boat-load of powder and other stores, voted to the service of Kentucky by the Virginia Assembly. He had experienced a long and exciting voyage from Pittsburg with this precious consignment, and about thirty of the settlers aided him in the perilous enterprise of transporting it overland to the stations on the Kentucky. While the ammunition was supposed to be used for defense, the greater part of it was necessarily spent in obtaining food. Without the great profusion of game the inhabitants must have starved; although several large crops of corn were raised, and some wheat, these were as yet insufficient for all.

Early in 1777 Indian "signs" began to multiply. McClellan's was now abandoned, leaving Boonesborough and Harrodsburg the only settlements maintained—except, perhaps, Price's, on the Cumberland, although Logan's Station was reoccupied in February. The number of men now in the country fit for duty did not exceed a hundred and fifty. In March the fighting men met at their respective stations and organized under commissioned officers; hitherto all military operations in Kentucky had been voluntary, headed by such temporary leaders as the men chose from their own number.

During the greater part of the year the palisaded stations were frequently attacked by the savages—Shawnese, Cherokees, and Mingos, in turn or in company. Some of these sieges lasted through several days, taxing the skill and bravery of the inhabitants to their utmost. Indian methods of attacking forts were far different from those that would be practised by white men. Being practically without military organization, each warrior acted largely on his own behalf. His object was to secrete himself, to kill his enemy, and if possible to bear away his scalp as a trophy. Every species of cover was taken advantage of—trees, stumps, bushes, hillocks, stones, furnished hiding-places. Feints were made to draw the attention of the garrison to one side, while the main body of the besiegers hurled themselves against the other. Having neither artillery nor scaling-ladders, they frequently succeeded in effecting a breach by setting fire to the walls. Pretending to retreat, they would lull the defenders into carelessness, when they would again appear from ambush, picking off those who came out for water, to attend to crops and cattle, or to hunt for food; often they exhibited a remarkable spirit of daring, especially when making a dash to secure scalps. Destroying crops, cattle, hogs, and poultry, stealing the horses for their own use, burning the outlying cabins, and guarding the trails against possible relief, they sought to reduce the settlers to starvation, and thus make them an easy prey. Every artifice known to besiegers was skilfully practised by these crafty, keen-eyed, quick-witted wilderness fighters, who seldom showed mercy. Only when white men aggressively fought them in their own manner could they be overcome.

In the last week of April, while Boone and Kenton were heading a sortie against a party of Shawnese besieging Boonesborough, the whites stumbled into an ambuscade, and Boone was shot in an ankle, the bone being shattered. Kenton, with that cool bravery for which this tall, vigorous backwoodsman was known throughout the border, rushed up, and killing a warrior whose tomahawk was lifted above the fallen man, picked his comrade up in his arms, and desperately fought his way back into the enclosure. It was several months before the captain recovered from this painful wound; but from his room he directed many a day-and-night defense, and laid plans for the scouting expeditions which were frequently undertaken throughout the region in order to discover signs of the lurking foe.

Being the larger settlement, Harrodsburg was more often attacked than Boonesborough, although simultaneous sieges were sometimes in progress, thus preventing the little garrisons from helping each other. At both stations the women soon became the equal of the men, fearlessly taking turns at the port-holes, from which little puffs of white smoke would follow the sharp rifle-cracks whenever a savage head revealed itself from behind bush or tree. When not on duty as marksmen, women were melting their pewter plates into bullets, loading the rifles and handing them to the men, caring for the wounded, and cooking whatever food might be obtainable. During a siege food was gained only by stealth and at great peril. Some brave volunteer would escape into the woods by night, and after a day spent in hunting, far away from hostile camps, return, if possible under cover of darkness, with what game he could find. It was a time to make heroes or cowards of either men or women—there was no middle course.

Amid this spasmodic hurly-burly there was no lack of marrying and giving in marriage. One day in early August, 1776, Betsey Calloway, the eldest of the captive girls, was married at Boonesborough to Samuel Henderson, one of the rescuing party—the first wedding in Kentucky. Daniel Boone, as justice of the peace, tied the knot. A diarist of the time has this record of a similar Harrodsburg event: "July 9, 1777.—Lieutenant Linn married—great merriment."

At each garrison, whenever not under actual siege, half of the men were acting as guards and scouts while the others cultivated small patches of corn within sight of the walls. But even this precaution sometimes failed of its purpose. For instance, one day in May two hundred Indians suddenly surrounded the corn-field at Boonesborough, and there was a lively skirmish before the planters could reach the fort.

Thus the summer wore away. In August Colonel Bowman arrived with a hundred militiamen from the Virginia frontier. A little later forty-eight horsemen came from the Yadkin country to Boone's relief, making so brave a display as they emerged from the tangled woods and in open order filed through the gates of the palisade, that some Shawnese watching the procession from a neighboring hill fled into Ohio with the startling report that two hundred Long Knife warriors had arrived from Virginia. In October other Virginians came, to the extent of a hundred expert riflemen; and late in the autumn the valiant Logan brought in from the Holston as much powder and lead as four packhorses could carry, guarded by a dozen sharpshooters, thus insuring a better prospect for food.

With these important supplies and reenforcements at hand the settlers were inspired by new hope. Instead of waiting for the savages to attack them, they thenceforth went in search of the savages, killing them wherever seen, thus seeking to outgeneral the enemy. These tactics quite disheartened the astonished tribesmen, and the year closed with a brighter outlook for the weary Kentuckians. It had been a time of constant anxiety and watchfulness. The settlers were a handful in comparison with their vigilant enemies. But little corn had been raised; the cattle were practically gone; few horses were now left; and on the twelfth of December Bowman sent word to Virginia that he had only two months' supply of bread for two hundred women and children, many of whom were widows and orphans. As for clothing, there was little to be had, although from the fiber of nettles a rude cloth was made, and deerskins were commonly worn.

CHAPTER XI

THE SIEGE OF BOONESBOROUGH

We have seen that Kentucky's numerous salt-springs lured wild animals thither in astonishing numbers; but for lack of suitable boiling-kettles the pioneers were at first dependent upon the older settlements for the salt needed in curing their meat. The Indian outbreak now rendered the Wilderness Road an uncertain path, and the Kentuckians were beginning to suffer from lack of salt—a serious deprivation for a people largely dependent upon a diet of game.

Late in the year 1777 the Virginia government sent out several large salt-boiling kettles for the use of the Western settlers. Both residents and visiting militiamen were allotted into companies, which were to relieve each other at salt-making until sufficient was manufactured to last the several stations for a year. It was Boone's duty to head the first party, thirty strong, which, with the kettles packed on horses, went to Lower Blue Licks early in January. A month passed, during which a considerable quantity of salt was made; several horse-loads had been sent to Boonesborough, but most of it was still at the camp awaiting shipment.

The men were daily expecting relief by the second company, when visitors of a different character appeared. While half of the men worked at the boiling, the others engaged in the double service of watching for Indians and obtaining food; of these was Boone. Toward evening of the seventh of February he was returning home from a wide circuit with his packhorse laden with buffalo-meat and some beaver-skins, for he had many traps in the neighborhood. A blinding snow-storm was in progress, which caused him to neglect his usual precautions, when suddenly he was confronted by four burly Shawnese, who sprang from an ambush. Keen of foot, he thought to outrun them, but soon had to surrender, for they shot so accurately that it was evident that they could kill him if they would.

The prisoner was conducted to the Shawnese camp, a few miles distant. There he found a hundred and twenty warriors under Chief Black Fish. Two Frenchmen, in English employ, were of the party; also two American renegades from the Pittsburg region, James and George Girty. These latter, with their brother Simon, had joined the Indians and, dressed and painted like savages, were assisting the tribesmen of the Northwest in raids against their fellow-borderers of Pennsylvania and Virginia. Boone was well known by reputation to all these men of the wilderness, reds and whites alike; indeed, he noticed that among the party were his captors of eight years before, who laughed heartily at again having him in their clutches.

He was loudly welcomed to camp, the Indians shaking his hands, patting him on the back, and calling him "brother"—for they always greatly enjoyed such exhibitions of mock civility and friendship—and the hunter himself pretended to be equally pleased at the meeting. They told him that they were on their way to attack Boonesborough, and wished him to lead them, but insisted that he first induce his fellow salt-makers to surrender. Boone thoroughly understood Indians; he had learned the arts of forest diplomacy, and although generally a silent man of action, appears to have been a plausible talker when dealing with red men. Knowing that only one side of the Boonesborough palisade had been completed, and that the war-party was five times as strong as the population of the hamlet, he thought to delay operations by strategy. He promised to persuade the salt-makers to surrender, in view of the overwhelming force and the promise of good treatment, and to go peacefully with their captors to the Shawnese towns north of the Ohio; and suggested that in the spring, when the weather was warmer, they could all go together to Boonesborough, and by means of horses comfortably remove the women and children. These would, under his persuasion, Boone assured his captors, be content to move to the North, and thenceforth either lived with the Shawnese as their adopted children or place themselves under British protection at Detroit, where Governor Hamilton offered

£20 apiece for American prisoners delivered to him alive and well.

The proposition appeared reasonable to the Indians, and they readily agreed to it. What would be the outcome Boone could not foretell. He realized, however, that his station was unprepared, that delay meant everything, in view of possible reenforcements from Virginia, and was willing that he and his comrades should stand, if need be, as a sacrifice—indeed, no other course seemed open. Going with his captors to the salt camp, his convincing words caused the men to stack their arms and accompany the savages, hoping thereby at least to save their families at Boonesborough from immediate attack.

The captives were but twenty-seven in number, some of the hunters not having returned to camp. Not all of the captors were, despite their promise, in favor of lenient treatment of the prisoners. A council was held, at which Black Fish, a chieftain of fine qualities, had much difficulty, through a session of two hours, in securing a favorable verdict. Boone was permitted to address the savage throng in explanation of his plan, his words being interpreted by a negro named Pompey, a fellow of some consequence among the Shawnese. The vote was close—fifty-nine for at once killing the prisoners, except Boone, and sixty-one for mercy; but it was accepted as decisive, and the store of salt being destroyed, and kettles, guns, axes, and other plunder packed on horses, the march northward promptly commenced.

Each night the captives were made fast and closely watched. The weather was unusually severe; there was much suffering from hunger, for the snow was deep, game scarce, and slippery-elm bark sometimes the only food obtainable. Descending the Licking, the band crossed the Ohio in a large boat made of buffalo-hides, which were stretched on a rude frame holding twenty persons; they then entered the trail leading to the Shawnese towns on the Little Miami, where they arrived upon the tenth day.

The prisoners were taken to the chief town of the Shawnese, Little Chillicothe, about three miles north of the present Xenia,

Ohio. There was great popular rejoicing, for not since Braddock's defeat had so many prisoners been brought into Ohio. Boone and sixteen of his companions, presumably selected for their good qualities and their apparent capacity as warriors, were now formally adopted into the tribe. Boone himself had the good fortune to be accepted as the son of Black Fish, and received the name Sheltowee (Big Turtle)—perhaps because he was strong and compactly built.

Adoption was a favorite method of recruiting the ranks of American tribes. The most tractable captives were often taken into the families of the captors to supply the place of warriors killed in battle. They were thereafter treated with the utmost affection, apparently no difference being made between them and actual relatives, save that, until it was believed that they were no longer disposed to run away, they were watched with care to prevent escape. Such was now Boone's experience. Black Fish and his squaw appeared to regard their new son with abundant love, and everything was done for his comfort, so far as was possible in an

Indian camp, save that he found himself carefully observed by day and night, and flight long seemed impracticable.

Boone was a shrewd philosopher. In his so-called "autobiography" written by Filson, he tells us that the food and lodging were "not so good as I could desire, but necessity made everything acceptable." Such as he obtained was, however, the lot of all. In the crowded, slightly built wigwams it was impossible to avoid drafts; they were filthy to the last degree; when in the home villages, there was generally an abundance of food—corn, hominy, pumpkins, beans, and game, sometimes all boiled together in the same kettle—although it was prepared in so slovenly a manner as to disgust even so hardy a man of the forest as our hero; the lack of privacy, the ever-present insects, the blinding smoke of the lodge-fire, the continual yelping of dogs, and the shrill, querulous tones of old women, as they haggled and bickered through the livelong day—all these and many other discomforts were intensely irritating to most white men. In order to disarm suspicion, Boone appeared to be happy. He whistled cheerfully at his tasks, learning what little there was left for him to learn of the arts of the warrior, sharing his game with his "father," and pretending not to see that he was being watched. At the frequent shooting-matches he performed just well enough to win the applause of his fellow braves, although, for fear of arousing jealousy, careful not to outdo the best of them. His fellow prisoners, less tactful, marveled at the ease with which their old leader adapted himself to the new life, and his apparent enjoyment of it. Yet never did he miss an opportunity to ascertain particulars of the intended attack on Boonesborough, and secretly planned for escape when the proper moment should arrive.

March was a third gone, when Black Fish and a large party of his braves and squaws went to Detroit to secure Governor Hamilton's bounty on those of the salt-makers who, from having acted in an ugly manner, had not been adopted into the tribe. Boone accompanied his "father," and frequently witnessed, unable to interfere, the whipping and "gauntlet-running" to which his unhappy fellow Kentuckians were subjected in punishment for their fractious behavior. He himself, early in his captivity, had been forced to undergo this often deadly ordeal; but by taking a dodging, zigzag course, and freely using his head as a battering-ram to topple over some of the warriors in the lines, had emerged with few bruises.*

Upon the arrival of the party at Detroit Governor Hamilton at once sent for the now famous Kentucky hunter and paid him many attentions. With the view of securing his liberty, the wily forest diplomat used the same sort of duplicity with the governor that had proved so effective with Black Fish. It was his habit to carry a leather bag fastened about his neck, containing his old commission as captain in the British colonial forces, signed by Lord Dunmore. This was for the

---

* Two lines of Indians were formed, five or six feet apart, on either side of a marked path. The prisoner was obliged to run between these lines, while there were showered upon him lusty blows from whatever weapons the tormentors chose to adopt—switches, sticks, clubs, and tomahawks. It required great agility, speed in running, and some aggressive strategy to arrive at the goal unharmed. Many white captives were seriously crippled in this thrilling experience, and not a few lost their lives.

purpose of convincing Indians, into whose hands he might fall, that he was a friend of the king; which accounts in a large measure for the tender manner in which they treated him. Showing the document to Hamilton as proof of his devotion to the British cause, he appears to have repeated his promise that he would surrender the people of Boonesborough and conduct them to Detroit, to live under British jurisdiction and protection. This greatly pleased the governor, who sought to ransom him from Black Fish for £100. But to this his "father" would not agree, stating that he loved him too strongly to let him go—as a matter of fact, he wished his services as guide for the Boonesborough expedition. Upon leaving for home, Hamilton presented Boone with a pony, saddle, bridle, and blanket, and a supply of silver trinkets to be used as currency among the Indians, and bade him remember his duty to the king.

Returning to Chillicothe with Black Fish, the hunter saw that preparations for the spring invasion of Kentucky were at last under way. Delawares, Mingos, and Shawnese were slowly assembling, and runners were carrying the war-pipe from village to village throughout Ohio. But while they had been absent at Detroit an event occurred which gave Black Fish great concern: one of the adopted men, Andrew Johnson—who had pretended among the Indians to be a simpleton, in order to throw off suspicion, but who in reality was one of the most astute of woodsmen—had escaped, carrying warning to Kentucky, and the earliest knowledge that reached the settlers of the location of the Shawnese towns. In May, Johnson and five comrades went upon a raid against one of these villages, capturing several horses and bringing home a bunch of Indian scalps, for scalping was now almost as freely practised by the frontiersmen as the savages; such is the degeneracy wrought by warlike contact with an inferior race. In June there was a similar raid by Boonesborough men, resulting to the tribesmen in large losses of lives and horses.

Upon the sixteenth of June, while Black Fish's party were boiling salt at the saline springs of the Scioto—about a dozen miles south of the present Chillicothe—Boone managed, by exercise of rare sagacity and enterprise, to escape the watchful eyes of his keepers, their attention having been arrested by the appearance of a huge flock of wild turkeys. He reached Boonesborough four days later after a perilous journey of a hundred and sixty miles through the forest, during which he had eaten but one meal—from a buffalo which he shot at Blue Licks. He had been absent for four and a half months, and Mrs. Boone, giving him up for dead, had returned with their family to her childhood home upon the Yadkin. His brother Squire, and his daughter Jemima—now married to Flanders Calloway—were the only kinsfolk to greet the returned captive, who appeared out of the woods as one suddenly delivered from a tomb.

During the absence of Daniel Boone there had been the usual Indian troubles in Kentucky. Colonel Bowman had just written to Colonel George Rogers Clark, "The Indians have pushed us hard this summer." But Clark himself at this time was gaining an important advantage over the enemy in his daring expedition against the British posts of Kaskaskia, Cahokia, and Vincennes, in the Illinois country. Realizing that there would be no end to Kentucky's trouble so long as the British, aided by their French-Canadian agents, were free to organize Indian armies north of the Ohio for the purpose of harrying the southern settlements, Clark "carried the war into Africa." With about a hundred and fifty men gathered from the frontiers of Virginia, Pennsylvania, and Kentucky, he descended the Ohio River, built a fort at Louisville, and by an heroic forced march across the country captured Kaskaskia, while Cahokia and Vincennes at once surrendered to the valorous Kentuckian.

Meanwhile there was business at hand for the people of Boonesborough. Amid all these alarms they had still neglected to complete their defenses; but now, under the energetic administration of Boone, the palisades were finished, gates and fortresses strengthened, and all four of the corner blockhouses put in order. In ten days they were ready for the slowly advancing host.

Unless fleeing, Indians are never in a hurry; they spend much time in noisy preparation. Hunters and scouts came into Boonesborough from time to time, and occasionally a retaliatory expedition would return with horses and scalps from the Little Miami and the Scioto, all of them reporting delays on the part of the enemy; nevertheless all agreed that a large force was forming. Toward the close of August Boone, wearied of being cooped up in the fort, went forth at the head of thirty woodsmen to scout in the neighborhood of the Scioto towns. With him were Kenton and Alexander Montgomery, who remained behind in Ohio to capture horses and probably prisoners, while Boone and the others returned after a week's absence. On their way home they discovered that the enemy was now at Lower Blue Licks, but a short distance from Boonesborough.

At about ten o'clock the following morning (September 7th) the Indian army appeared before the fort. It numbered fully four hundred warriors, mostly Shawnese, but with some Wyandots, Cherokees, Delawares, Mingos, and other tribesmen. Accompanying them were some forty French-Canadians, all under the command of Boone's "father," the redoubtable Black Fish. Pompey served as chief interpreter.

Much time was spent in parleys, Boone in this manner delaying operations as long as possible, vainly hoping that promised reenforcements might meanwhile arrive from the Holston. Black Fish wept freely, after the Indian fashion, over the ingratitude of his runaway "son," and his present stubborn attitude; for the latter now told the forest chief that he and his people proposed to fight to the last man. Black Fish presented letters and proclamations from Hamilton, again offering pardon to all who would take the oath of allegiance to the king, and military offices for Boone and the other leaders. When these were rejected, the Indians attempted treachery, seeking to overpower and kill the white commissioners to a treaty being held in front of the fort. From this final council, ending in a wild uproar, in which bullets flew and knives and tomahawks clashed, the whites escaped with difficulty, the two Boones and another commissioner receiving painful wounds.

A siege of ten days now ensued (September 8th to 17th), one of the most remarkable in the history of savage warfare. The site of the fort, a parallelogram embracing three-quarters of an acre, had been unwisely chosen. There was abundant cover for the enemy under the high river bank, also beneath an encircling clay bank rising from the salt-lick branch; from hills upon either side spies could see what was happening within the walls, and occasionally drop a ball into the small herd of cattle and horses sheltered behind the palisades; while to these natural disadvantages were added the failure of the garrison to clear from the neighborhood of the walls the numerous trees, stumps, bushes, and rocks, each of which furnished the best of cover for a lurking foe.

Such, however, was the stubbornness of the defense, in which the women were, in their way, quite as efficient as the men, that the forces under Black Fish could make but small impression upon the valiant little garrison. Every artifice known to savages, or

CLIMAX OF THE TREATY.

Indians and British agents treacherously attack treaty commissioners. (See pp. 161, 162.) Reduced from Ranck's "Boonesborough."

that could be suggested by the French, was without avail. Almost nightly rains and the energy of the riflemen frustrated the numerous attempts to set fire to the cabins by throwing torches and lighted fagots upon their roofs; a tunnel, intended to be used for blowing up the walls, was well under way from the river bank when rain caused it to cave in; attempts at scaling were invariably repelled, and in sharpshooting the whites as usual proved the superiors.

But the result often hung in the balance. Sometimes the attack lasted throughout the night, the scene being constantly lighted by the flash of the rifles and the glare of hurling fagots. Besiegers and garrison frequently exchanged fierce cries of threat and defiance, mingled with many a keen shaft of wit and epithet; at times the yells and whoops of the savages, the answering shouts and huzzahs of the defenders, the screams of women and girls, the howling of dogs, the snorting and bellowing of the plunging live stock, together with the sharp rattle of firearms, created a deafening hubbub well calculated to test the nerves of the strongest.

At last, on the morning of Friday, the eighteenth, the Indians, now thoroughly disheartened, suddenly disappeared into the forest as silently as they had come. Again Boonesborough was free, having passed through the longest and severest ordeal of attack ever known in Kentucky; indeed, it proved to be the last effort against this station. Within the walls sixty persons had been capable of bearing arms, but only forty were effective, some of these being negroes; Logan's Fort had sent a reenforcement of fifteen men, and Harrodsburg a few others. Of the garrison but two were killed and four wounded, while Boone estimated that the enemy lost thirty-seven killed and a large number wounded. The casualties within the fort were astonishingly small, when the large amount of ammunition expended by the besiegers is taken into account. After they had retired, Boone's men picked up a hundred and twenty-five pounds of flattened bullets that had been fired at the log stronghold, handfuls being scooped up beneath the portholes of the bastions; this salvage made no account of the balls thickly studding the walls, it being estimated that a hundred pounds of lead were buried in the logs of one of the bastions.

A week later a small company of militiamen arrived from Virginia, and several minor expeditions were now made against the Shawnese upon their own soil. These raids were chiefly piloted by Boone's salt-makers, many of whom had now returned from captivity. Boone is credited with saying in his later years, although no doubt in ruder language than this: "Never did the Indians pursue so disastrous a policy as when they captured me and my salt-boilers, and taught us, what we did not know before, the way to their towns and the geography of their country; for though at first our captivity was considered a great calamity to Kentucky, it resulted in the most signal benefits to the country."

Captain Boone was not without his critics. Soon after the siege he was arraigned before a court-martial at Logan's Fort upon the following charges preferred by Colonel Calloway, who thought that the great hunter was in favor of the British Government and had sought opportunity to play into its hands, therefore should be deprived of his commission in the Kentucky County militia:

"1. That Boone had taken out twenty-six men * to make salt at the Blue Licks, and the Indians had caught him trapping for beaver ten miles below on Licking, and he voluntarily surrendered his men at the Licks to the enemy.

"2. That when a prisoner, he engaged with Gov. Hamilton to surrender the people of Boonesborough to be removed to Detroit, and live under British protection and jurisdiction.

"3. That returning from captivity, he encouraged a party of men to accompany him to the Paint Lick Town, weakening the garrison at a time when the arrival of an Indian army was daily expected to attack the fort.

"4. That preceding the attack on Boonesborough, he was willing to take the officers of the fort, on pretense of making peace, to

* Account is only taken, in these charges, of the twenty-seven captives.

the Indian camp, beyond the protection of the guns of the garrison."

Boone defended himself at length, maintaining that he aimed only at the interests of the country; that while hunting at the licks he was engaged in the necessary service of the camp; that he had used duplicity to win the confidence of the enemy, and it resulted favorably, as he was thereby enabled to escape in time to warn his people and put them in a state of defense; that his Scioto expedition was a legitimate scouting trip, and turned out well; and that in the negotiations before the fort he was simply "playing" the Indians in order to gain time for expected reenforcements. He was not only honorably acquitted, but at once advanced to the rank of major, and received evidences of the unhesitating loyalty of all classes of his fellow borderers, the majority of whom appear to have always confided in his sagacity and patriotism.

Personally vindicated, the enemy departed, and several companies of militia now arriving to garrison the stations for the winter, Major Boone once more turned his face to the Yadkin and sought his family. He found them at the Bryan settlement, living comfortably in a small log cabin, but until then unconscious of his return from the wilderness in which they had supposed he found his grave.

CHAPTER XII

SOLDIER AND STATESMAN

In Daniel Boone's "autobiography," he dismisses his year of absence from Kentucky with few words: "I went into the settlement, and nothing worthy of notice passed for some time." No doubt he hunted in some of his old haunts upon the Yadkin; and there is reason for believing that he made a trip upon business of some character to Charleston, S. C.

Meanwhile, his fellow settlers of Kentucky had not been inactive. In February (1779) Clark repossessed himself of Vincennes after one of the most brilliant forced marches of the Revolution; and having there captured Governor Hamilton—the "hair-buying general," as the frontiersmen called him, because they thought he paid bounties on American scalps—had sent him a prisoner to Virginia. The long siege of Boonesborough and the other attacks of the preceding year, together with more recent assaults upon flatboats descending the Ohio, had strongly disposed the Kentuckians to retaliate on the Shawnese. Two hundred and thirty riflemen under Colonel Bowman rendezvoused in July at the mouth of the Licking, where is now the city of Covington. Nearly a third of the force were left to guard the boats in which they crossed the Ohio, the rest marching against Old Chillicothe, the chief Shawnese town on the Little Miami. They surprised the Indians, and a hotly contested battle ensued, lasting from dawn until ten o'clock in the morning; but the overpowering numbers of the savages caused Bowman to return crestfallen to Kentucky with a loss of nearly a dozen men. This was the forerunner of many defeats of Americans, both bordermen and regulars, at the hands of the fierce tribesmen of Ohio.

Readers of Revolutionary history as related from the Eastern standpoint are led to suppose that the prolonged struggle with the mother country everywhere strained the resources of the young nation, and was the chief thought of the people. This high tension was, however, principally in the tide-water region. In the "back country," as the Western frontiers were called, there was no lack of patriotism, and bordermen were numerous in the colonial armies; yet the development of the trans-Alleghany region was to them of more immediate concern, and went forward vigorously, especially during the last half of the war. This did not mean that the backwoodsmen of the foot-hills were escaping from the conflict by crossing westward beyond the mountains; they were instead planting themselves upon the left flank, for French and Indian scalping parties were continually harrying the Western settlements, and the Eastern forces were too busily engaged to give succor. Kentuckians were left practically alone to defend the back-door of the young Republic.

In this year (1779) the Virginia legislature adopted laws for the preemption of land in Kentucky, which promised a more secure tenure than had hitherto prevailed, and thus gave great impetus to over-mountain emigration. Hitherto those going out to Kentucky were largely hunters, explorers, surveyors, and land speculators; comparatively few families were established in the wilderness stations. But henceforth the emigration was chiefly by households, some by boats down the Ohio River, and others overland by the Wilderness Road—for the first official improvement of which Virginia made a small appropriation at this time. Says Chief Justice Robinson,* whose parents settled in Kentucky in December:

"This beneficent enactment brought to the country during the fall and winter of that year an unexampled tide of emigrants, who, exchanging all the comforts of their native society and homes for settlements for themselves and their children here, came like pilgrims to a wilderness to be made secure by their arms and habitable by the toil of their lives. Through privations incredible and perils thick, thousands of men, women, and children came in successive caravans, forming continuous streams of human beings, horses, cattle, and other domestic animals, all moving onward along a lonely and house-

---

* Address at Camp Madison, Franklin County, Ky., in 1843.

less path to a wild and cheerless land. Cast your eyes back on that long procession of missionaries in the cause of civilization; behold the men on foot with their trusty guns on their shoulders, driving stock and leading packhorses; and the women, some walking with pails on their heads, others riding, with children in their laps, and other children swung in baskets on horses, fastened to the tails of others going before; see them encamped at night expecting to be massacred by Indians; behold them in the month of December, in that ever-memorable season of unprecedented cold called the 'hard winter,' traveling two or three miles a day, frequently in danger of being frozen, or killed by the falling of horses on the icy and almost impassable trace, and subsisting on stinted allowances of stale bread and meat; but now, lastly, look at them at the destined fort, perhaps on the eve of merry Christmas, when met by the hearty welcome of friends who had come before, and cheered by fresh buffalo-meat and parched corn, they rejoice at their deliverance, and resolve to be contented with their lot."

In October, as a part of this great throng, Daniel Boone and his family returned to Kentucky by his old route through Cumberland Gap, being two weeks upon the journey. The great hunter was at the head of a company of Rowan County folk, and carried with him two small cannon, the first artillery sent by Virginia to protect the Western forts. Either as one of his party, or later in the season, there came to Kentucky Abraham Lincoln, of Rockingham County, Va., grandfather of the martyred president. The Lincolns and the Boones had been neighbors and warm friends in Pennsylvania, and ever since had maintained pleasant relations—indeed, had frequently intermarried. It was by Boone's advice and encouragement that Lincoln migrated with his family to the "dark and bloody ground" and took up a forest claim in the heart of Jefferson County. Daniel's younger brother Edward, killed by Indians a year later, was of the same company.

Boone also brought news that the legislature had incorporated "the town of Boonesborough in the County of Kentuckey,"

SITE OF BOONESBOROUGH TO-DAY.

Fort site, to which roadway leads, is hidden by foliage on the left; the ridge in the background faced and overlooked the fort. Reduced from Ranck's "Boonesborough."

of which he was named a trustee, which office he eventually declined. The town, although now laid out into building lots, and anticipating a prosperous growth, never rose to importance and at last passed away. Nothing now remains upon the deserted site, which Boone could have known, save a decrepit sycamore-tree and a tumble-down ferry established in the year of the incorporation.

As indicated in Robinson's address, quoted above, the winter of 1779–80 was a season of unwonted severity. After an exceptionally mild autumn, cold weather set in by the middle of November and lasted without thaw for two months, with deep snow and zero temperature. The rivers were frozen as far south as Nashville; emigrant wagons were stalled in the drifts while crossing the mountains, and everywhere was reported unexampled hardship. It will be remembered that the Revolutionary Army in the East suffered intensely from the same cause. The Indians had, the preceding summer, destroyed most of the corn throughout Kentucky; the game was rapidly decreasing, deer and buffaloes having receded before the advance of settlement, and a temporary famine ensued. Hunters were employed to obtain meat for the newcomers; and in this occupation Boone and Harrod, in particular, were actively engaged throughout the winter, making long trips into the forest, both north and south of Kentucky River.

The land titles granted by the Transylvania Company having been declared void, it became necessary for Boone and the other settlers under that grant to purchase from the State government of Virginia new warrants. For this purpose Boone set out for Richmond in the spring. Nathaniel and Thomas Hart and others of his friends commissioned him to act as their agent in this matter. With his own small means and that which was entrusted to him for the purpose, he carried $20,000 in depreciated paper money—probably worth but half that amount in silver. It appears that of this entire sum he was robbed upon his way—where, or under what circumstances, we are unable to discover. His petition to the Kentucky legislature, in his old age, simply states the fact of the robbery, adding that he "was left destitute." A large part of the money was the property of his old friends, the Harts, but many others also suffered greatly. There was some disposition on the part of a few to attribute dishonorable action to Boone; but the Harts, although the chief losers, came promptly to the rescue and sharply censured his critics, declaring him to be a "just and upright" man, beyond suspicion—a verdict which soon became unanimous. Sympathy for the honest but unbusinesslike pioneer was so general, that late in June, soon after the robbery, Virginia granted him a preemption of a thousand acres of land in what is now Bourbon County.

A tradition exists that while in Virginia that summer Boone called upon his former host at Detroit, then a prisoner of war, and expressed sympathy for the sad plight into which the English governor had fallen; also some indignation at the harsh treatment accorded him, and of which Hamilton bitterly complained.

The founder of Boonesborough was soon back at his station, for he served as a juryman there on the first of July. During his absence immigration into Kentucky had been greater than ever; three hundred well-laden family boats had arrived in the spring from the Pennsylvania and New York frontiers, while many caravans had come from Virginia and the Carolinas over the Wilderness Road. Attacks by Indian scalping parties had been numerous along both routes, but particularly upon the Ohio. As a reprisal for Bowman's expedition of the previous year, and intending to interrupt settlement, Colonel Byrd, of the British Army, descended in June upon Ruddle's and Martin's Stations, at the forks of the Licking, with six hundred Indians and French-Canadians, and bringing six small cannon with which to batter the Kentucky palisades. Both garrisons were compelled to surrender, and the victors returned to Detroit with a train of three hundred prisoners—men, women, and children—upon whom the savages practised cruelties of a particularly atrocious character.

This inhuman treatment of prisoners of war created wide-spread indignation upon the American border. In retaliation, George

Rogers Clark at once organized an expedition to destroy Pickaway, one of the principal Shawnese towns on the Great Miami. The place was reduced to ashes and a large number of Indians killed, the Americans losing seventeen men. Clark had previously built Fort Jefferson, upon the first bluff on the eastern side of the Mississippi below the mouth of the Ohio, in order to accentuate the claim of the United States that it extended to the Mississippi on the west; but as this was upon the territory of friendly Chickasaws, the invasion aroused their ire, and it was deemed prudent temporarily to abandon the post.

Another important event of the year (November, 1780) was the division of Kentucky by the Virginia legislature into three counties—Jefferson, with its seat at Louisville, now the chief town in the Western country; Lincoln, governed from Harrodsburg; and Fayette, with Lexington as its seat. Of these, Fayette, embracing the country between the Kentucky and the Ohio, was the least populated; and, being the most northern and traversed by the Licking River, now the chief war-path of the Shawnese, was most exposed to attack. After his return Boone soon tired of Boonesborough, for in his absence the population had greatly changed by the removal or death of many of his old friends; and, moreover, game had quite deserted the neighborhood. With his family, his laden packhorses, and his dogs, he therefore moved to a new location across Kentucky River, about five miles northwest of his first settlement. Here, at the crossing of several buffalo-trails, and on the banks of Boone's Creek, he built a palisaded log house called Boone's Station. Upon the division of Kentucky this new stronghold fell within the borders of Fayette County.

In the primitive stage of frontier settlement, when the common weal demanded from every man or boy able to carry a rifle active militia service whenever called upon, the military organization was quite equal in importance to the civil. The new wilderness counties were therefore equipped with a full roll of officers, Fayette County's colonel being John Todd, while Daniel Boone was lieutenant-colonel; Floyd, Pope, Logan, and

Trigg served the sister counties in like manner. The three county regiments were formed into a brigade, with Clark as brigadier-general, his headquarters being at Louisville (Fort Nelson). Each county had also a court to try civil and criminal cases, but capital offenses could only be tried at Richmond. There was likewise a surveyor for each county, Colonel Thomas Marshall serving for Fayette; Boone was his deputy for several years (1782–85).

In October, 1780, Edward Boone, then but thirty-six years of age, accompanied Daniel to Grassy Lick, in the northeast part of the present Bourbon County, to boil salt. Being attacked by a large band of Indians, Edward was killed in the first volley, and fell at the feet of his brother, who at once shot the savage whom he thought to be the slayer. Daniel then fled, stopping once to load and kill another foe. Closely pursued, he had recourse to all the arts of evasion at his command—wading streams to break the trail, swinging from tree to tree by aid of wild grape-vines, and frequently zigzagging. A hound used in the chase kept closely to him, however, and revealed his whereabouts by baying, until the hunter killed the wily beast, and finally reached his station in safety. Heading an avenging party of sixty men, Boone at once went in pursuit of the enemy, and followed them into Ohio, but the expedition returned without result.

The following April Boone went to Richmond as one of the first representatives of Fayette County in the State legislature. With the approach of Cornwallis, La Fayette, whose corps was then protecting Virginia, abandoned Richmond, and the Assembly adjourned to Charlottesville. Colonel Tarleton, at the head of a body of light horse, made a dash upon the town, hoping to capture the law-makers, and particularly Governor Jefferson, whose term was just then expiring. Jefferson and the entire Assembly had been warned, but had a narrow escape (June 4th), for while they were riding out of one end of town Tarleton was galloping in at the other. The raider succeeded in capturing three or four of the legislators, Boone among them, and after destroying a quantity of military stores took his prisoners to Cornwallis's camp. The members were paroled after a few days' detention. The Assembly fled to Staunton, thirty-five miles distant, where it resumed the session. The released members are reported to have again taken their seats, although, after his capture, Boone's name does not appear in the printed journals. Possibly the conditions of the parole did not permit him again to serve at the current session, which closed the twenty-third of June. He seems to have spent the summer in Kentucky, and late in September went up the Ohio to Pittsburg, thence journeying to the home of his boyhood in eastern Pennsylvania, where he visited friends and relatives for a month, and then returned to Richmond to resume his legislative duties.

Of all the dark years which Kentucky experienced, 1782 was the bloodiest. The British authorities at Detroit exerted their utmost endeavors to stem the rising tide of settlement and to crush the aggressive military operations of Clark and his fellow-borderers. With presents and smooth words they enlisted the cooperation of the most distant tribes, the hope being held out that success would surely follow persistent attack and a policy of "no quarter." It would be wearisome to cite all the forays made by savages during this fateful year, upon flatboats descending the Ohio, upon parties of immigrants following the Wilderness Road, upon outlying forest settlers, and in the neighborhood of fortified stations. The border annals of the time abound in details of robbery, burning, murder, captivities, and of heart-rending tortures worse than death. A few only which have won prominence in history must here suffice.

In March, some Wyandots had been operating in the neighborhood of Boonesborough and then departed for Estill's Station, fifteen miles away, near the present town of Richmond. Captain Estill and his garrison of twenty-five men were at the time absent on a scout, and thus unable to prevent the killing and scalping of a young woman and the capture of a negro slave. According to custom, the Indians retreated rapidly after this adventure, but were pursued by Estill. A stubborn fight ensued, there being now eighteen whites and twenty-five savages. Each man stood behind a tree, and through nearly two hours fought with uncommon tenacity. The Indians lost seventeen killed and two wounded, while the whites were reduced to three survivors, Estill himself being among the slain. The survivors then withdrew by mutual consent.

In May, his station having been attacked with some loss, Captain Ashton followed the retreating party of besiegers, much larger than his own squad, and had a fierce engagement with them lasting two hours. He and eleven of his comrades lost their lives, and the remainder fled in dismay. A similar tragedy occurred in August, when Captain Holden, chasing a band of scalpers, was defeated with a loss of four killed and one wounded.

The month of August marked the height of the onslaught. Horses were carried off, cattle killed, men at work in the fields mercilessly slaughtered, and several of the more recent and feeble stations were abandoned. Bryan's Station, consisting of forty cabins enclosed by a stout palisade, was the largest and northernmost of a group of

Fayette County settlements in the rich country of which Lexington is the center. An army of nearly a thousand Indians—the largest of either race that had thus far been mustered in the West—was gathered under Captains Caldwell and McKee, of the British Army, who were accompanied by the renegade Simon Girty and a small party of rangers. Scouts had given a brief warning to the little garrison of fifty riflemen, but when the invaders appeared during the night of August 15th the defenders were still lacking a supply of water.

The Indians at first sought to conceal their presence by hiding in the weeds and bushes which, as at Boonesborough, had carelessly been left standing. Although aware of the extent of the attacking force, the garrison affected to be without suspicion. In the morning the women and girls, confident that if no fear were exhibited they would not be shot by the hiding savages, volunteered to go to the spring outside the walls, and by means of buckets bring in enough water to fill the reservoir. This daring feat was successfully accomplished. Although painted faces and gleaming rifles could readily be seen in the underbrush all about the pool, this bucket-line of brave frontierswomen laughed and talked as gaily as if unconscious of danger, and were unmolested.

Immediately after their return within the gates, some young men went to the spring to draw the enemy's fire, and met a fusillade from which they barely escaped with their lives. The assault now began in earnest. Runners were soon spreading the news of the invasion among the neighboring garrisons. A relief party of forty-six hurrying in from Lexington fell into an ambush and lost a few of their number in killed and wounded, but the majority reached the fort through a storm of bullets. The besiegers adopted the usual methods of savage attack—quick rushes, shooting from cover, fire-arrows, and the customary uproar of whoops and yells—but without serious effect. The following morning, fearful of a general outpouring of settlers, the enemy withdrew hurriedly and in sullen mood.

Colonel Boone was soon marching through the forest toward Bryan's, as were similar companies from Lexington, McConnell's, and McGee's, the other members of the Fayette County group; and men from the counties of Jefferson and Lincoln were also upon the way, under their military leaders. The neighboring contingents promptly arrived at Bryan's in the course of the afternoon.

The next morning a hundred and eighty-two of the best riflemen in Kentucky, under Colonel Todd as ranking officer, started in pursuit of the foe, who had followed a buffalo-trail to Blue Licks, and were crossing the Licking when the pursuers arrived on the scene. A council of war was held, at which Boone, the most experienced man in the party, advised delay until the expected reenforcements could arrive. The bulk of the Indians had by this time escaped, leaving only about three hundred behind, who were plainly luring the whites to an attack. Todd, Trigg, and most of the other leaders sided with Boone; but Major Hugh McGary, an ardent, hot-headed man, with slight military training, dared the younger men to follow him, and spurred his horse into the river, whither, in the rash enthusiasm of the moment, the hot-bloods followed him, leaving the chief officers no choice but to accompany them.

Rushing up a rocky slope on the other side, where a few Indians could be seen, the column soon fell into an ambush. A mad panic resulted, in which the Kentuckians for the most part acted bravely and caused many of the enemy to fall; but they were overpowered and forced to flee in hot haste, leaving seventy of their number dead on the field and seven captured. Among the killed were Todd and Trigg, fighting gallantly to the last. Boone lost his son Israel, battling by his side, and himself escaped only by swimming the river amid a shower of lead. A day or two later Logan arrived with four hundred men, among whom was Simon Kenton, to reenforce Todd; to him was left only the melancholy duty of burying the dead, now sadly disfigured by Indians, vultures, and wolves.

The greater part of the savage victors, laden with scalps and spoils, returned exultantly to their northern homes, although small bands still remained south of the Ohio, carrying wide-spread devastation through the settlements, especially in the neighborhood of Salt River, where, at one station, thirty-seven prisoners were taken.

While all these tragedies were being enacted, General Clark, at the Falls of the Ohio, had offered only slight aid. But indignant protests sent in to the Virginia authorities by the Kentucky settlers, who were now in a state of great alarm, roused the hero of Kaskaskia and Vincennes to a sense of his duty. A vigorous call to arms was now issued throughout the three counties. Early in November over a thousand mounted riflemen met their brigadier at the mouth of the Licking, and from the site of Cincinnati marched through the Ohio forests to the Indian towns on the Little Miami. The savages fled in consternation, leaving the Kentuckians to burn their cabins and the warehouses of several British traders, besides large stores of grain and dried meats, thus entailing great suffering among the Shawnese during the winter now close at hand.

The triumphant return of this expedition

gave fresh heart to the people of Kentucky; and the sequel proved that, although the tribesmen of the north frequently raided the over-mountain settlers throughout the decade to come, no such important invasions as those of 1782 were again undertaken.

CHAPTER XIII

KENTUCKY'S PATH OF THORNS

THE preliminary articles of peace between the United States and Great Britain had been signed on the thirtieth of November, 1782; but it was not until the following spring that the news reached Kentucky. The northern tribes had information of the peace quite as early; and discouraged at apparently losing their British allies, who had fed, clothed, armed, and paid them from headquarters in Detroit, for a time suspended their organized raids into Kentucky. This welcome respite caused immigration to increase rapidly.

We have seen how the old system of making preemptions and surveys led to the overlapping of claims, the commission of many acts of injustice, and wide-spread confusion in titles. Late in 1782, Colonel Thomas Marshall, the surveyor of Fayette County, arrived from Virginia, and began to attempt a straightening of the land conflict. Boone was now not only the surveyor's deputy, but both sheriff and county lieutenant of Fayette, a combination of offices which he held until his departure from Kentucky. It was his duty as commandant to provide an escort for Marshall through the woods to the Falls of the Ohio, where was now the land-office. The following order which he issued for this guard has been preserved; it is a characteristic sample of the many scores of letters and other documents which have come down to us from the old hero, who fought better than he spelled:

"Orders to Capt. Hazelrigg—your are amedetly to order on Duty 3 of your Company as goude [guard] to scorte Col Marshshall to the falls of ohigho you will call on those who was Exicused from the Shone [Shawnese] Expedistion and those who Come into the County after the army Marched they are to meet at Lexinton on Sunday next with out fale given under my hand this 6 Day of Janury 1783.

"DNL BOONE"

Another specimen document of the time has reference to the scouting which it was necessary to maintain throughout much of the year; for small straggling bands of the enemy were still lurking about, eager to capture occasional scalps, the proudest trophies which a warrior could obtain. It also is apparently addressed to Hazelrigg:

"orders the 15th feberry 1783

"Sir you are amedetly to Call on Duty one thurd of our melitia as will mounted on horse as poseble and Eight Days purvistion to take a touere as follows Commanded by Leut Col patison and Rendevues at Strod [Strode's Station] on thusday the 20th from there to March to Colkes [Calk's] Cabin thence an Este Corse till the gat 10 miles above the uper Blew Licks then Down to Lickes thence to Limestown and if no Sine [is] found a stright Corse to Eagel Crick 10 miles from the head from then home if Sine be found the Commander to act as he thinks most prudent as you will be the Best Judge when on the Spot. You will first Call on all who [were] Excused from the Expedistion

Except those that went to the falls with Col. Marshall and then Call them off as they Stand on the List here in faile not. given und my hand

"DANIEL BOONE C Lt."

In March the Virginia legislature united the three counties into the District of Kentucky, with complete legal and military machinery; in the latter, Benjamin Logan ranked as senior colonel and district lieutenant. It will be remembered that when the over-mountain country was detached from Fincastle, it was styled the County of Kentucky; then the name of Kentucky was obliterated by its division into three counties; and now the name was revived by the creation of the district, which in due time was to become a State. The log-built town of Danville was named as the capital.

It is estimated that during the few years immediately following the close of the Revolutionary War several thousand persons came each year to Kentucky from the seaboard States, although many of these returned to their homes either disillusioned or because of Indian scares. In addition to the actual settlers, who cared for no more land than they could use, there were merchants who saw great profits in taking boat-loads of goods down the Ohio or by pack-trains over the mountains; lawyers and other young professional men who wished to make a start in new communities; and speculators who hoped to make fortunes in obtaining for a song extensive tracts of fertile wild land, which they vainly imagined would soon be salable at large prices for farms and town sites. Many of the towns, although ill-kept and far from prosperous in appearance, were fast extending beyond their lines of palisade and boasting of stores, law-offices, market-places, and regular streets; Louisville had now grown to a village of three hundred inhabitants, of whom over a third were fighting-men. Besides Americans, there were among the newcomers many Germans, Scotch, and Irish, thrifty in the order named.

At last Kentucky was raising produce more than sufficient to feed her own people, and an export trade had sprung up. Crops were being diversified: Indian corn still remained the staple, but there were also melons, pumpkins, tobacco, and orchards; besides, great droves of horses, cattle, sheep, and hogs, branded or otherwise marked, ranged at large over the country, as in old days on the Virginia and Carolina foot-hills. Away from the settlements buffaloes still yielded much beef, bacon was made from bears, and venison was a staple commodity.

The fur trade was chiefly carried on by French trappers; but American hunters, like the Boones and Kenton, still gathered peltries from the streams and forests, and took or sent them to the East, either up the Ohio in bateaux or on packhorses over the mountains—paths still continually beset by savage assailants. Large quantities of ginseng were also shipped to the towns on the seaboard. Of late there had likewise developed a considerable trade with New Orleans and other Spanish towns down the Mississippi River. Traders with flatboats laden with Kentucky produce—bacon, beef, salt, and tobacco—would descend the great waterway, both of whose banks were audaciously claimed by Spain as far up as the mouth of the Ohio, and take great risks from Indian attack or from corrupt Spanish custom-house officials, whom it was necessary to bribe freely that they might not confiscate boat and cargo. This commerce was always uncertain, often ending in disaster, but immensely profitable to the unprincipled men who managed to ingratiate themselves with the Spanish authorities.

Boone was now in frequent demand as a pilot and surveyor by capitalists who relied upon his unrivaled knowledge of the country to help them find desirable tracts of land; often he was engaged to meet incoming parties of immigrants over the Wilderness Road, with a band of riflemen to guard them against Indians, to furnish them with wild meat—for the newcomers at first were inexpert in killing buffaloes—and to show them the way to their claims. He was prominent as a pioneer; as county lieutenant he summoned his faithful men-at-arms to repel or avenge savage attacks; and his fame as hunter and explorer had by this time not only become general throughout the United States but had even reached Europe.

His reputation was largely increased by the appearance in 1784 of the so-called "autobiography." We have seen that, although capable of roughly expressing himself on paper, and of making records of his rude surveys, he was in no sense a scholar. Yet this autobiography, although signed by himself, is pedantic in form, and deals in words as large and sonorous as though uttered by the great Doctor Samuel Johnson. As a matter of fact, it is the production of John Filson, the first historian of Kentucky and one of the pioneers of Cincinnati. Filson was a schoolmaster, quite devoid of humor, and with a strong penchant for learned phrases. In setting down the story of Boone's life, as related to him by the great hunter, he made the latter talk in the first person, in a stilted manner quite foreign to the hardy but unlettered folk of whom Boone was a type. Wherever Boone's memory failed, Filson appears to have filled in the gaps from tradition and his own imagination; thus the autobiography is often wrong as to facts, and possesses but minor value as historical material. The little book was, however, widely circulated both at home and abroad, and gave Boone a notoriety excelled by few men of his day. Some years later Byron wrote some indifferent lines upon "General Boone of Kentucky;" the public journals of the time had accounts of his prowess, often grossly exaggerated; and English travelers into the interior of America eagerly sought the hero and told of him in their books.

Yet it must be confessed that he had now ceased to be a real leader in the affairs of Kentucky. A kindly, simple-hearted, modest, silent man, he had lived so long by himself alone in the woods that he was ill fitted to cope with the horde of speculators and other self-seekers who were now despoiling the old hunting-grounds to which Finley had piloted him only fifteen years before. Of great use to the frontier settlements as explorer, hunter, pilot, land-seeker, surveyor, Indian fighter, and sheriff—and, indeed, as magistrate and legislator so long as Kentucky was a community of riflemen—he had small capacity for the economic and political sides of commonwealth-building. For this reason we find him hereafter, although still in middle life, taking but slight part in the making of Kentucky; none the less did his career continue to be adventurous, picturesque, and in a measure typical of the rapidly expanding West.

Probably in the early spring of 1786 Boone left the neighborhood of the Kentucky River, and for some three years dwelt at Maysville (Limestone), still the chief gateway to Kentucky for the crowds of immigrants who came by water. He was there a tavern-keeper—probably Mrs. Boone was the actual hostess—and small river merchant. He still frequently worked at surveying, of course hunted and trapped as of old, and traded up and down the Ohio River between Maysville and Point Pleasant—the last-named occupation a far from peaceful one, for in those troublous times navigation of the Ohio was akin to running the gauntlet; savages haunted the banks, and by dint of both strategy and open attack wrought a heavy mortality among luckless travelers and tradesmen. The goods which he bartered to the Kentuckians for furs, skins, and ginseng were obtained in Maryland, whither he and his sons went with laden pack-animals, often driving before them loose horses for sale in the Eastern markets. Sometimes they followed some familiar mountain road, at others struck out over new paths, for no longer was the Wilderness Road the only overland highway to the West.

Kentucky was now pursuing a path strewn with thorns. Northward, the British still held the military posts on the upper lakes, owing to the non-fulfilment of certain stipulations in the treaty of peace. Between these and the settlements south of the Ohio lay a wide area populated by powerful and hostile tribes of Indians, late allies of the British, deadly enemies of Kentucky, and still aided and abetted by military agents of the king. To the South, Spain controlled the Mississippi, the commercial highway of the West; jealous of American growth, she harshly denied to Kentuckians the freedom of the river, and was accused of turning against them and their neighbors of Tennessee the fierce warriors of the Creek and Cherokee tribes. On their part, the Kentuckians looked with hungry eyes upon the rich lands held by Spain.

Not least of Kentucky's trials was the political discontent among her own people, which for many years lay like a blight upon her happiness and prosperity. Virginia's home necessities had prevented that commonwealth from giving much aid to the West during the Revolution, and at its conclusion her policy toward the Indians lacked the aggressive vigor for which Kentuckians pleaded. This was sufficient cause for dissatisfaction; but to this was added another of still greater importance. To gain the free navigation of the Mississippi, and thus to have an outlet to the sea, long appeared to be essential to Western progress. At first the Eastern men in Congress failed to realize this need, thereby greatly exasperating the over-mountain men. All manner of schemes were in the air, varying with men's temperaments and ambitions. Some, like Clark—who, by this time had, under the influence of intemperance, greatly fallen in popular esteem, although not without followers—favored a filibustering expedition against the Spanish;

and later (1788), when this did not appear practicable, were willing to join hands with Spain herself in the development of the continental interior; and later still (1793–94), to help France oust Spain from Louisiana. Others wished Kentucky to be an independent State, free to conduct her own affairs and make such foreign alliances as were needful; but Virginia and Congress did not release her.

Interwoven with this more or less secret agitation for separating the West from the East were the corrupt intrigues of Spain, which might have been more successful had she pursued a persistent policy. Her agents —among whom were some Western pioneers who later found difficulty in explaining their conduct—craftily fanned the embers of discontent, spread reports that Congress intended to sacrifice to Spain the navigation rights of the West, distributed bribes, and were even accused of advising Spain to arm the Southern Indians in order to increase popular uneasiness over existing conditions. Spain also offered large land grants to prominent American borderers who should lead colonies to settle beyond the Mississippi and become her subjects—a proposition which Clark once offered to accept, but did not; but of which we shall see that Daniel Boone, in his days of discontent, took advantage, as did also a few other Kentucky pioneers. Ultimately Congress resolved never to abandon its claim to the Mississippi (1787); and when the United States became strong, and the advantages of union were more clearly seen in the West, Kentucky became a member of the sisterhood of States (1792).

It is estimated that, between 1783 and 1790, fully fifteen hundred Kentuckians were massacred by Indians or taken captive to the savage towns; and the frontiers of Virginia and Pennsylvania furnished their full quota to the long roll of victims. It is impossible in so small a volume as this to mention all of even the principal incidents in the catalogue of assaults, heroic defenses, murders, burnings, torturings, escapes, reprisals, and ambushes which constitute the lurid annals of this protracted border warfare. The reader who has followed thus far this story of a strenuous life, will understand what these meant; to what deeds of daring they gave rise on the part of the men and women of the border; what privation and anguish they entailed. But let us not forget that neither race could claim, in this titanic struggle for the mastery of the hunting-grounds, a monopoly of courage or of cowardice, of brutality or of mercy. The Indians suffered quite as keenly as the whites in the burning of their villages, crops, and supplies, and by the loss of life either in battle, by stealthy attack, or by treachery. The frontiersmen learned from the red men the lessons of forest warfare, and often outdid their tutors in ferocity. The contest between civilization and savagery is, in the nature of things, unavoidable; the result also is foreordained. It is well for our peace of mind that, in the dark story of the Juggernaut car, we do not inquire too closely into details.

In 1785, goaded by numerous attacks on settlers and immigrants, Clark led a thousand men against the tribes on the Wabash; but by this time he had lost control of the situation, and cowardice on the part of his troops, combined with lack of provisions, led to the practical failure of the expedition, although the Indians were much frightened.

At the same time, Logan was more successful in an attack on the Shawnese of the Scioto Valley, who lost heavily in killed and prisoners. In neither of these expeditions does Boone appear to have taken part.

The year 1787 was chiefly notable, in the history of the West, for the adoption by Congress of the Ordinance for the government of the Territory Northwest of the River Ohio, wherein there dwelt perhaps seven thousand whites, mostly unprogressive French-Canadians, in small settlements flanking the Mississippi and the Great Lakes, and in the Wabash Valley. Along the Ohio were scattered a few American hamlets, chiefly in Kentucky. In the same year the Indian war reached a height of fury which produced a panic throughout the border, and frantic appeals to Virginia, which brought insufficient aid. Boone, now a town trustee of Maysville, was sent to the legislature that autumn, and occupied his seat at Richmond from October until

January. While there, we find him strongly complaining that the arms sent out to Kentucky by the State during the year were unfit for use, the swords being without scabbards, and the rifles without cartridge-boxes or flints.

A child of the wilderness, Boone was law-abiding and loved peace, but he chafed at legal forms. He had, in various parts of Kentucky, preempted much land in the crude fashion of his day, both under the Transylvania Company and the later statutes of Virginia—how much, it would now be difficult to ascertain. In his old survey-books, still preserved in the Wisconsin State Historical Library, one finds numerous claim entries for himself, ranging from four hundred to ten thousand acres each—a tract which he called "Stockfield," near Boonesborough; on Cartwright's Creek, a branch of Beech Fork of Salt River; on the Licking, Elkhorn, Boone's Creek, and elsewhere. The following is a specimen entry, dated "Aperel the 22 1785," recording a claim made "on the Bank of Cantuckey"; it illustrates the loose surveying methods of the time: "Survayd for Dal Boone 5000 acres begin at Robert Camels N E Corner at at 2 White ashes and Buckeyes S 1200 p[oles] to 3 Shuger trees Ealm and walnut E 666 p to 6 Shuger trees and ash N 1200 p to a poplar and beech W 666 p to the begining."

It did not occur to our easy-going hero that any one would question his right to as much land as he cared to hold in a wilderness which he had done so much to bring to the attention of the world. But claim-jumpers were no respecters of persons. It was discovered that Boone had carelessly failed to make any of his preemptions according to the letter of the law, leaving it open for any adventurer to reenter the choice claims which he had selected with the care of an expert, and to treat him as an interloper. Suits of ejectment followed one by one (1785–98), until in the end his acres were taken from him by the courts, and the good-hearted, simple fellow was sent adrift in the world absolutely landless.

At first, when his broad acres began to melt away, the great hunter, careless of his possessions, appeared to exhibit no concern;

but the accumulation of his disasters, together with the rapid growth of settlement upon the hunting-grounds, and doubtless some domestic nagging, developed within him an intensity of depression which led him to abandon his long-beloved Kentucky and vow never again to dwell within her limits. In the autumn of 1788, before his disasters were quite complete, this resolution was carried into effect; with wife and family, and what few worldly goods he possessed, he removed to Point Pleasant, at the junction of the Great Kanawha and the Ohio—in our day a quaint little court-house town in West Virginia.

CHAPTER XIV

IN THE KANAWHA VALLEY

During his early years on the Kanawha, Boone kept a small store at Point Pleasant. Later, he moved to the neighborhood of Charleston, where he was engaged in the usual variety of occupations—piloting immigrants; as deputy surveyor of Kanawha County, surveying lands for settlers and speculators; taking small contracts for victualing the militia, who were frequently called out to protect the country from Indian forays; and in hunting. Some of his expeditions took him to the north of the Ohio, where he had several narrow escapes from capture and death at the hands of the enemy, and even into his old haunts on the Big Sandy, the Licking, and the Kentucky.

He traveled much, for a frontiersman. In 1788 he went with his wife and their son Nathan by horseback to the old Pennsylvania home in Berks County, where they spent a month with kinsfolk and friends. We find him in Maysville, on a business trip, during the year; indeed, there are evidences of numerous subsequent visits to that port. In May of the following year he was on the Monongahela River with a drove of horses for sale, Brownsville then being an important market for ginseng, horses, and cattle; and in the succeeding July he writes to a client, for whom he had done some surveying, that he would be in Philadelphia during the coming winter.

In October, 1789, there came to him, as the result of a popular petition, the appointment of lieutenant-colonel of Kanawha County—the first military organization in the valley; and in other ways he was treated with marked distinction by the primitive border folk of the valley, both because of his brilliant career in Kentucky and the fact that he was a surveyor and could write letters. One who knew him intimately at this time has left a pleasing description of the man, which will assist us in picturing him as he appeared to his new neighbors: "His large head, full chest, square shoulders, and stout form are still impressed upon my mind. He was (I think) about five feet ten inches in height, and his weight say 175. He was solid in mind as well as in body, never frivolous, thoughtless, or agitated; but was always quiet, meditative, and impressive, unpretentious, kind, and friendly in his manner. He came very much up to the idea we have of the old Grecian philosophers—particularly Diogenes."

By the summer of 1790, Indian raids again became almost unbearable. Fresh robberies and murders were daily reported in Kentucky, and along the Ohio and the Wabash. The expedition of Major J. F. Hamtramck, of the Federal Army, against the tribesmen on the Wabash, resulted in the burning of a few villages and the destruction of much corn; but Colonel Josiah Harmar's expedition in October against the towns on the Scioto and the St. Joseph, at the head of nearly 1,500 men, ended in failure and a crushing defeat, although the Indian losses were so great that the army was allowed to return to Cincinnati unmolested. Boone does not appear to have taken part in these operations, his militiamen probably being needed for home protection.

The following year the General Government for the first time took the field against the Indians in earnest. For seven years it had attempted to bring the tribesmen to terms by means of treaties, but without avail. Roused to fury by the steady increase of settlement north as well as south of the Ohio, the savages were making life a torment to the borderers. War seemed alone the remedy. In June, General Charles Scott, of Kentucky, raided the Miami and Wabash Indians. Two months later General James Wilkinson, with five hundred Kentuckians, laid waste a Miami village and captured many prisoners. These were intended but to open the road for an expedition of far greater proportions. In October, Governor Arthur St. Clair, of the Northwest Territory, a broken-down man unequal to such a task, was despatched against the Miami towns with an ill-organized army of two thousand raw troops. Upon the fourth of November they were surprised near the principal Miami village; hundreds of the men fled at the first alarm, and of those who remained over six hundred fell during the engagement, while nearly three hundred were wounded. This disastrous termination of the campaign demoralized the West and left the entire border again open to attack—an advantage which the scalping parties did not neglect.

While this disaster was occurring, Boone was again sitting in the legislature at Richmond, where he represented Kanawha County from October 17th to December 20th. The journals of the Assembly show him to have been a silent member, giving voice only in yea and nay; but he was placed upon two then important committees—religion, and propositions and licenses. It was voted to send ammunition for the militia on the Monongahela and the Kanawha, who were to be called out for the defense of the frontier. Before leaving Richmond, Boone wrote as follows to the governor:

"Monday 13th Decr 1791

"Sir as sum purson Must Carry out the armantstion [ammunition] to Red Stone [Brownsville, Pa.,] if your Exclency should have thought me a proper purson I would undertake it on conditions I have the apintment to vitel the company at Kanhowway [Kanawha] so that I Could take Down the flowre as I paste that place I am your Excelenceys most obedent omble servant

"DAL BOONE."

Five days later the contract was awarded to him; and we find among his papers receipts, obtained at several places on his way home, for the lead and flints which he was to deliver to the various military centers. But the following May, Colonel George Clendennin sharply complains to the governor that the ammunition and rations which Boone was to have supplied to Captain Caperton's rangers had not yet been delivered, and that Clendennin was forced to purchase these supplies from others. It does not appear from the records how this matter was settled; but as there seems to have been no official inquiry, the non-delivery was probably the result of a misunderstanding.

At last, after a quarter of a century of bloodshed, the United States Government was prepared to act in an effective manner. General Anthony Wayne—"Mad Anthony," of Stony Point—after spending a year and a half in reorganizing the Western army, established himself, in the winter of 1793–94, in a log fort at Greenville, eighty miles north of Cincinnati, and built a strong outpost at Fort Recovery, on the scene of St. Clair's defeat. After resisting an attack on Fort Recovery made on the last day of June by over two thousand painted warriors from the Upper Lakes, he advanced with his legion of about three thousand well-disciplined troops to the Maumee Valley and built Fort Defiance. Final battle was given to the tribesmen on the twentieth of August at Fallen Timbers. As the result of superb charges by infantry and cavalry, in forty minutes the Indian army was defeated and scattered. The backbone of savage opposition to Northwestern settlement was broken, and at the treaty of Greenville in the following summer (1795) a peace was secured which remained unbroken for fifteen years.

Wayne's great victory over the men of the wilderness gave new heart to Kentucky and the Northwest. The pioneers were exuberant in the expression of their joy. The long war, which had lasted practically since the mountains were first crossed by Boone and Finley, had been an almost constant strain upon the resources of the country. Now no longer pent up within palisades, and expecting nightly to be awakened by the whoops of savages to meet either slaughter or still more dreaded captivity, men could go forth without fear to open up forests, to cultivate fields, and peaceably to pursue the chase.

To hunters like Boone, in particular, this great change in their lives was a matter for rejoicing. The Kanawha Valley was not as rich in game as he had hoped; but in Kentucky and Ohio were still large herds of buffaloes and deer feeding on the cane-brake and the rank vegetation of the woods, and resorting to the numerous salt-licks which had as yet been uncontaminated by settlement.

After the peace, Boone for several seasons devoted himself almost exclusively to hunting; in beaver-trapping he was especially successful, his favorite haunt for these animals being the neighboring Valley of the Gauley. His game he shared freely with neighbors, now fast increasing in numbers, and the skins and furs were shipped to market, overland or by river, as of old.

Upon removing to the Kanawha, he still had a few claims left in Kentucky, but suits for ejectment were pending over most of these. They were all decided against him, and the remaining lands were sold by the sheriff for taxes, the last of them going in 1798. His failure to secure anything for his children to inherit, was to the last a source of sorrow to Boone.

The Kanawha in time came to be distasteful to him. Settlements above and below were driving away the game, and sometimes his bag was slight; the crowding of population disturbed the serenity which he sought in deep forests; the nervous energy of these newcomers, and the avarice of some of them, annoyed his quiet, hospitable soul; and he fretted to be again free, thinking that civilization cost too much in wear and tear of spirit.

Boone had long looked kindly toward the broad, practically unoccupied lands of forest and plain west of the Mississippi. Adventurous hunters brought him glowing tales of buffaloes, grizzly bears, and beavers to be found there without number. Spain, fearing an assault upon her possessions from Canada, was just now making flattering offers to those American pioneers who should colonize her territory, and by casting their fortunes with her people strengthen them. This opportunity attracted the disappointed man; he thought the time ripe for making a move which should leave the crowd far behind, and comfortably establish him in a country wherein a hunter might, for many years to come, breathe fresh air and follow the chase untrammeled.

In 1796, Daniel Morgan Boone, his oldest son, traveled with other adventurers in boats to St. Charles County, in eastern Missouri, where they took lands under certificates of cession from Charles Dehault Delassus, the Spanish lieutenant-governor of Upper Louisiana, resident at St. Louis. There were four families, all settling upon Femme Osage

Creek, six miles above its junction with the Missouri, some twenty-five miles above the town of St. Charles, and forty-five by water from St. Louis.

Thither they were followed, apparently in the spring of 1799, by Daniel Boone and wife and their younger children. The departure of the great hunter, now in his sixty-fifth year, was the occasion for a general gathering of Kanawha pioneers at the home near Charleston. They came on foot, by horseback, and in canoe, from far and near, and bade him a farewell as solemnly affectionate as though he were departing for another world; indeed, Missouri then seemed almost as far away to the West Virginians as the Klondike is to dwellers in the Mississippi basin to-day—a long journey by packhorse or by flatboat into foreign wilds, beyond the great waterway concerning which the imaginations of untraveled men often ran riot.

The hegira of the Boones, from the junction of the Elk and the Kanawha, was accomplished by boats, into which were crowded such of their scant herd of live stock as could be accommodated. Upon the way they stopped at Kentucky towns along the Ohio, either to visit friends or to obtain provisions, and attracted marked attention, for throughout the West Boone was, of course, one of the best-known men of his day. In Cincinnati he was asked why, at his time of life, he left the comforts of an established home again to subject himself to the privations of the frontier. "Too crowded!" he replied with feeling. "I want more elbow-room!"

Arriving at the little Kentucky colony on Femme Osage Creek, where the Spanish authorities had granted him a thousand arpents * of land abutting his son's estate upon the north, he settled down in a little log cabin erected largely by his own hands, for the fourth and last time as a pioneer. He was never again in the Kanawha Valley, and but twice in Kentucky—once to testify as to some old survey-marks made by him, and again to pay the debts which he had left when removing to Point Pleasant.

---

* Equivalent to about 845 English acres.

CHAPTER XV

A SERENE OLD AGE

MISSOURI'S sparse population at that time consisted largely of Frenchmen, who had taken easily to the yoke of Spain. For a people of easy-going disposition, theirs was an ideal existence. They led a patriarchal life, with their flocks and herds grazing upon a common pasture, and practised a crude agriculture whose returns were eked out by hunting in the limitless forests hard by. For companionship, the crude log cabins in the little settlements were assembled by the banks of the waterways, and there was small disposition to increase tillage beyond domestic necessities. There were practically no taxes to pay; military burdens sat lightly; the local syndic (or magistrate), the only government servant to be met outside of St. Louis, was sheriff, judge, jury, and commandant combined; there were no elections, for representative government was unknown;

the fur and lead trade with St. Louis was the sole commerce, and their vocabulary did not contain the words enterprise and speculation.

Here was a paradise for a man of Boone's temperament, and through several years to come he was wont to declare that, next to his first long hunt in Kentucky, this was the happiest period of his life. On the eleventh of July, 1800, Delassus—a well-educated French gentleman, and a good judge of character—appointed him syndic for the Femme Osage district, a position which the old man held until the cession of Louisiana to the United States. This selection was not only because of his prominence among the settlers and his recognized honesty and fearlessness, but for the reason that he was one of the few among these unsophisticated folk who could make records. In a primitive community like the Femme Osage, Boone may well have ranked as a man of some education; and certainly he wrote a bold, free hand, showing much practise with the pen, although we have seen that his spelling and grammar might have been improved. When the government was turned over to President Jefferson's commissioner,

BOONE'S CABIN IN ST. CHARLES COUNTY, MISSOURI.

From photograph in possession of Wisconsin State Historical Society.

Delassus delivered to that officer, by request, a detailed report upon the personality of his subordinates, and this is one of the entries in the list of syndics: "Mr. Boone, a respectable old man, just and impartial, he has already, since I appointed him, offered his resignation owing to his infirmities—believing I know his probity, I have induced him to remain, in view of my confidence in him, for the public good."

Boone's knowledge did not extend to law-books, but he had a strong sense of justice; and during his four years of office passed upon the petty disputes of his neighbors with such absolute fairness as to win popular approbation. His methods were as primitive and arbitrary as those of an Oriental pasha; his penalties frequently consisted of lashes on the bare back "well laid on;" he would observe no rules of evidence, saying he wished only to know the truth; and sometimes both parties to a suit were compelled to divide the costs and begone. The French settlers had a fondness for taking their quarrels to court; but the decisions of the good-hearted syndic of Femme Osage, based solely upon common sense in the rough, were respected as if coming from a supreme bench. His contemporaries said that in no other office ever held by the great rifleman did he give such evidence of undisguised satisfaction, or display so great dignity as in this rôle of magistrate. Showing newly arrived American immigrants to desirable tracts of land was one of his most agreeable duties; when thus tendering the hospitalities of the country to strangers, it was remarked that our patriarch played the Spanish "don" to perfection.

In October, 1800, Spain agreed to deliver Louisiana to France; but the latter found it impracticable at that time to take possession of the territory. By the treaty of April 30, 1803, the United States, long eager to secure for the West the open navigation of the Mississippi, purchased the rights of France. It was necessary to go through the form, both in New Orleans and in St. Louis, of transfer by Spain to France, and then by France to the United States. The former ceremony took place in St. Louis, the capital of Upper Louisiana, upon the ninth of

March, 1804, and the latter upon the following day. Daniel Boone's authority as a Spanish magistrate ended when the flag of his adopted country was hauled down for the last time in the Valley of the Mississippi.

The coming of the Americans into power was welcomed by few of the people of Louisiana. The French had slight patience with the land-grabbing temper of the "Yankees," who were eager to cut down the forests, to open up farms, to build towns, to extend commerce, to erect factories—to inaugurate a reign of noise and bustle and avarice. Neither did men of the Boone type—who had become Spanish subjects in order to avoid the crowds, to get and to keep cheap lands, to avoid taxes, to hunt big game, and to live a simple Arcadian life—at all enjoy this sudden crossing of the Mississippi River, which they had vainly hoped to maintain as a perpetual barrier to so-called progress.

Our hero soon had still greater reason for lamenting the advent of the new *régime.* His sad experience with lands in Kentucky had not taught him prudence. When the United States commission came to examine the titles of Louisiana settlers to the claims which they held, it was discovered that Boone had failed properly to enter the tract which had been ceded to him by Delassus. The signature of the lieutenant-governor was sufficient to insure a temporary holding, but a permanent cession required the approval of the governor at New Orleans; this Boone failed to obtain, being misled, he afterward stated, by the assertion of Delassus that so important an officer as a syndic need not take such precautions, for he would never be disturbed. The commissioners, while highly respecting him, were regretfully obliged under the terms of the treaty to dispossess the old pioneer, who again found himself landless. Six years later (1810) Congress tardily hearkened to his pathetic appeal, backed by the resolutions of the Kentucky legislature, and confirmed his Spanish grant in words of praise for "the man who has opened the way to millions of his fellow men."

By the time he was seventy years old, Boone's skill as a hunter had somewhat lessened. His eyes had lost their phenomenal strength; he could no longer perform those nice feats of marksmanship for which in his prime he had attained wide celebrity, and rheumatism made him less agile. But as a trapper he was still unexcelled, and for many years made long trips into the Western wilderness, even into far-off Kansas, and at least once (1814, when eighty years old) to the great game fields of the Yellowstone. Upon such expeditions, often lasting several months, he was accompanied by one or more of his sons, by his son-in-law Flanders Calloway, or by an old Indian servant who was sworn to bring his master back to the Femme Osage dead or alive—for, curiously enough, this wandering son of the wilderness ever yearned for a burial near home.

Beaver-skins, which were his chief desire, were then worth nine dollars each in the St. Louis market. He appears to have amassed a considerable sum from this source, and from the sale of his land grant to his sons, and in 1810 we find him in Kentucky paying his debts. This accomplished, tradition says that he had remaining only fifty cents; but he gloried in the fact that he was at last "square with the world," and returned to Missouri exultant.

The War of 1812–15 brought Indian troubles to this new frontier, and some of the farm property of the younger Boones was destroyed in one of the savage forays. The old man fretted at his inability to assist in the militia organization, of which his sons Daniel Morgan and Nathan were conspicuous leaders; and the state of the border did not permit of peaceful hunting. In the midst of the war he deeply mourned the death of his wife (1813)—a woman of meek, generous, heroic nature, who had journeyed over the mountains with him from North Carolina, and upon his subsequent pilgrimages, sharing all his hardships and perils, a proper helpmeet in storm and calm.

Penniless, and a widower, he now went to live with his sons, chiefly with Nathan, then forty-three years of age. After being first a hunter and explorer, and then an industrious and successful farmer, Nathan had won distinction in the war just closed and entered the regular army, where he reached the rank of lieutenant-colonel and had a wide and thrilling experience in Indian fighting. Daniel Morgan is thought to have been the first set-

NATHAN BOONE'S HOUSE IN ST. CHARLES COUNTY, MISSOURI.

tler in Kansas (1827); A. G. Boone, a grandson, was one of the early settlers of Colorado, and prominently connected with Western Indian treaties and Rocky Mountain exploration; and another grandson of the great Kentuckian was Kit Carson, the famous scout for Frémont's transcontinental expedition.

It was not long before the Yankee *régime* confirmed Boone's fears. The tide of immigration crossed the river, and rolling westward again passed the door of the great Kentuckian, driving off the game and monopolizing the hunting-grounds. Laws, courts, politics, speculation, and improvements were being talked about, to the bewilderment of the French and the unconcealed disgust of the former syndic. Despite his great age, he talked strongly of moving still farther West, hoping to get beyond the reach of settlement; but his sons and neighbors persuaded him against it, and he was obliged to accommodate himself as best he might to the new conditions. In summer he would work on the now substantial and prosperous farms of his children, chopping trees for the winter's wood. But at the advent of autumn the spirit of restlessness seized him, when he would take his canoe, with some relative or his Indian servant, and disappear up the Missouri and its branches for weeks together. In 1816, we hear of him as being at Fort Osage, on his way to the Platte, "in the dress of the roughest, poorest hunter." Two years later, he writes to his son Daniel M.: "I intend by next autumn to take two or three whites and a party of Osage Indians to visit the salt mountains, lakes, and ponds and see these natural curiosities. They are about five or six hundred miles west of here" —presumably the rock salt in Indian Territory; it is not known whether this trip was taken. He was greatly interested in Rocky Mountain exploration, then much talked of, and eagerly sought information regarding California; and was the cause of several young men migrating thither. A tale of new lands ever found in him a delighted listener.

In these his declining years, although he had suffered much at the hands of the world, Boone's temperament, always kindly, mellowed in tone. Decay came gradually, without palsy or pain; and, amid kind friends and an admiring public, his days passed in tranquillity. The following letter written by him at this period to his sister-in-law Sarah (Day) Boone, wife of his brother Samuel, is characteristic of the man, and gives to us, moreover, probably the only reliable account we possess of his religious views:

"october the 19th 1816

"Deer Sister

"With pleasuer I Rad a Later from your sun Samuel Boone who informs me that you are yett Liveing and in good health Considing your age I wright to you to Latt you know I have Not forgot you and to inform you of my own Situation sence the Death of your Sister Rabacah I Leve with flanders Calaway But am at present at my sun Nathans and in tolarabel halth you Can gass at my feilings by your own as we are So Near one age I Need Not write you of our satuation as Samuel Bradley or James grimes Can inform you of Every Surcomstance Relating to our famaly and how we

Leve in this World and what Chance we shall have in the next we know Not for my part I am as ignerant as a Child all the Relegan I have to Love and fear god beleve in Jeses Christ Don all the good to my Nighbour and my self that I Can and Do as Little harm as I Can help and trust on gods marcy for the Rest and I Beleve god neve made a man of my prisepel to be Lost and I flater my self Deer sister that you are well on your way in Cristeanaty gave my Love to all your Childran and all my frends fearwell my Deer sister

"DANIEL BOONE

"Mrs. Sarah Boone

"N B I Red a Later yesterday from sister Hanah peninton by hir grand sun Da[l] Ringe she and all hir Childran are Well at present

"D B"

Many strangers of distinction visited him at Nathan's home near the banks of the Missouri, and the public journals of the day always welcomed an anecdote of the great hunter's prowess—although most of the stories which found their way into print were

Deer Sister octtober the 19 1816

With pleasuer I Red a Later from
your Sun Samuel Boone who informs me that
you are yett Leving and in good helth Considering
your age I wright to you to Latt you Know I have
Not forgot you and to inform you of my own Situation
Sence the Death of your Sister Rabacah I Leve
with flanders Calaway But am at present at
my Sun Nathans and in tolarabel helth
you Can gass at my feelings by your own as
we are So Near one age I Need Not write you
of our Satuation as Samuel Bradley or James
grimes Can inform you of Every Surcomstance
Relating to our famaly and how we Leve in this
World and what Chance we Shall have in the next we
know Not for my part I am as ignerant as a Child
all the Relegan I have to Love and fear god beleve
in Jeses Christ Dow all the good to my Neighbour
and my Self that I Can and Do as Little harm

BOONE'S RELIGIOUS VIEWS.

Reduced facsimile from original MS. in possession of Wisconsin State Historical Society.

as I can help and trust on god's mercy for the Rest and I Beleve god neve made a man of my prinsibel to be Lost and I flater my Self Dear Sister that you are well on your way in Cristianaty gave my Love to all your Childran and all my frends fearwell my Dear Sister

Mrs

Sarah Boone

Daniel Boone

N B

I Red a Later yesterday from Sister Hanah peninton by hir grand Sun Dal Ringe She and all hir Childran are Well at presant

D B

either deliberate inventions or unconsciously exaggerated traditions. From published descriptions of the man by those who could discriminate, we may gain some idea of his appearance and manner. The great naturalist Audubon once passed a night under a West Virginia roof in the same room with Boone, whose "extraordinary skill in the management of a rifle" is alluded to. He says: "The stature and general appearance of this wanderer of the Western forests approached the gigantic. His chest was broad and prominent; his muscular powers displayed themselves in every limb; his countenance gave indication of his great courage, enterprise, and perseverance; and when he spoke the very motion of his lips brought the impression that whatever he uttered could not be otherwise than strictly true. I undressed, whilst he merely took off his hunting-shirt and arranged a few folds of blankets on the floor, choosing rather to lie there, as he observed, than on the softest bed."

Timothy Flint, one of his early biographers, knew the "grand old man" in Missouri, and thus pictures him: "He was five feet ten inches in height, of a very erect, clean-limbed, and athletic form—admirably fitted in structure, muscle, temperament, and habit for the endurance of the labors, changes, and sufferings he underwent. He had what phrenologists would have considered a model head—with a forehead peculiarly high, noble, and bold—thin and compressed lips—a mild, clear, blue eye—a large and prominent chin, and a general expression of countenance in which fearlessness and courage sat enthroned, and which told the beholder at a glance what he had been and was formed to be." Flint declares that the busts, paintings, and engravings of Boone bear little resemblance to him. "They want the high port and noble daring of his countenance. . . . Never was old age more green, or gray hairs more graceful. His high, calm, bold forehead seemed converted by years into iron."

Rev. James E. Welch, a revivalist, thus tells of Boone as he saw him at his meetings in 1818: "He was rather low of stature, broad shoulders, high cheek-bones, very mild countenance, fair complexion, soft and quiet in his manner, but little to say unless spoken to, amiable and kind in his feelings, very fond of quiet retirement, of cool self-possession and indomitable perseverance. He never made a profession of religion, but still was what the world calls a very moral man."

In 1819, the year before the death of Boone, Chester Harding, an American portrait-painter of some note, went out from St. Louis to make a life study of the aged Kentuckian. He found him at the time "living alone in a cabin, a part of an old blockhouse," evidently having escaped for a time from the conventionalities of home life, which palled upon him. The great man was roasting a steak of venison on the end of his ramrod. He had a marvelous memory of the incidents of early days, although forgetful of passing events. "I asked him," says Harding, "if he never got lost in his long wanderings after game? He said 'No, I was never lost, but I was bewildered once for three days.'" The portrait is now in the possession of the painter's grandson, Mr. William H. King, of Winnetka, Ill. Harding says that he "never finished the drapery of the original picture, but copied the head, I think, at three different times." It is from this portrait (our frontispiece), made when Boone was an octogenarian, emaciated and feeble—although not appearing older than seventy years—that most others have been taken; thus giving us, as Flint says, but a shadowy notion of how the famous explorer looked in his prime. There is in existence, however, a portrait made by Audubon, from memory—a charming picture, representing Boone in middle life.*

* The story of the original Harding portrait, as gathered from statements to the present writer by members of the painter's family, supplemented by letters of Harding himself to the late Lyman C. Draper, is an interesting one. The artist used for his portrait a piece of ordinary table oil-cloth. For many years the painting was in the capitol at Frankfort, Ky., "from the fact that it was hoped the State would buy it." But the State had meanwhile become possessed of another oil portrait painted about 1839 or 1840 by a Mr. Allen, of Harrodsburg, Ky.—an ideal sketch, of no special merit. Harding's portrait, apparently the only one of Boone painted from life, was not purchased, for the State did not wish to be at the expense of two paintings. Being upon a Western trip, in 1861, Harding, then an old man and a resident of Springfield, Mass., rescued his portrait, which was in bad condition, and carried it home. The process of restoration was necessarily a vigorous one. The artist writes (October 6, 1861): "The picture had been banged about until the greater part of it was broken to pieces. . . . The head is as perfect as when

Serene and unworldly to the last, and with slight premonition of the end, Daniel Boone passed from this life upon the twenty-sixth of September, 1820, in the eighty-sixth year of his age. The event took place in the home of his son Nathan, said to be the first stone house built in Missouri. The convention for drafting the first constitution of the new State was then in session in St. Louis. Upon learning the news, the commonwealth-builders adjourned for the day in respect to his memory; and as a further mark of regard wore crape on their left arms for twenty days. The St. Louis Gazette, in formally announcing his death, said: "Colonel Boone was a man of common stature, of great en-

it was painted, in color, though there are some small, almost imperceptible, cracks in it." The head and neck, down to the shirt-collar, were cut out and pasted upon a full-sized canvas; on this, Harding had "a very skilful artist" repaint the bust, drapery, and background, under the former's immediate direction. The picture in the present state is, therefore, a composite. The joining shows plainly in most lights. Upon the completion of the work, Harding offered to sell it to Draper, but the negotiation fell through. The restored portrait was then presented by the artist to his son-in-law, John L. King, of Springfield, Mass., and in due course it came into the possession of the latter's son, the present owner.

terprise, strong intellect, amiable disposition, and inviolable integrity—he died universally regretted by all who knew him. . . . Such is the veneration for his name and character."

Pursuant to his oft-repeated request, he was buried by the side of his wife, upon the bank of Teugue Creek, about a mile from the Missouri. There, in sight of the great river of the new West, the two founders of Boonesborough rested peacefully. Their graves were, however, neglected until 1845, when the legislature of Kentucky made a strong appeal to the people of Missouri to allow the bones to be removed to Frankfort, where, it was promised, they should be surmounted by a fitting monument. The eloquence of Kentucky's commissioners succeeded in overcoming the strong reluctance of the Missourians, and such fragments as had not been resolved into dust were removed amid much display. But in their new abiding-place they were again the victims of indifference; it was not until 1880, thirty-five years later, that the present monument was erected.

BOONE'S MONUMENT AT FRANKFORT, KENTUCKY.

A Serene Old Age

We have seen that Daniel Boone was neither the first explorer nor the first settler of Kentucky. The trans-Alleghany wilds had been trodden by many before him; even he was piloted through Cumberland Gap by Finley, and Harrodsburg has nearly a year's priority over Boonesborough. He had not the intellect of Clark or of Logan, and his services in the defense of the country were of less importance than theirs. He was not a constructive agent of civilization. But in the minds of most Americans there is a pathetic, romantic interest attaching to Boone that is associated with few if any others of the early Kentuckians. His migrations in the vanguard of settlement into North Carolina, Kentucky, West Virginia, and Missouri, each in their turn; his heroic wanderings in search of game and fresh lands; his activity and numerous thrilling adventures during nearly a half-century of border warfare; his successive failures to acquire a legal foothold in the wilderness to which he had piloted others; his persistent efforts to escape the civilization of which he had been the forerunner; his sunny temper amid trials of the sort that made of Clark a plotter and a misanthrope; his sterling integrity; his serene old age—all these have conspired to make for Daniel Boone a place in American history as one of the most lovable and picturesque of our popular heroes; indeed, the typical backwoodsman of the trans-Alleghany region.

INDEX

Index

Index

Index

Index

Index

Index

Index

(1)